Facing Fear Head On

Edited by
Jackie Parry and Shelley Wright

Published in Australia in 2018 by SisterShip Press Pty Ltd
Part of SisterShip Magazine, NSW, Australia
www.sistershippress.com

Typset and Cover Design by Shellack Designers
Printed and bound in Australia by SisterShip Press Pty Ltd

National Library of Australia data:

SisterShip Press Pty Ltd, 2018, Facing Fear Head On

ISBN: 978-0-6484283-1-2

Also available as an ebook

In collaboration with SisterShip Magazine

www.sistershippress.com
www.sistershipmagazine.com

For everyone courageous enough to admit they feel fear.

Contents

Foreword

My heart jack-knifed in my chest as the boat bucked beneath me. I was alone in the frigid Southern Ocean and my boat had just shattered as the mast came crashing down. I was facing the horrible realisation that I might not live past the next five minutes as another wall of white water slammed into the boat, taking my breath away. Shaking with fear I needed to act. I needed to survive. Four hours of hell later and I knew that I was going to make it. I was going to live to see the sunrise.

That horrendous demasting, as I sailed solo around Antarctica, was terrifying and something that I hope no one else needs to live through, but I didn't fully understand the ramifications of that night until months later. I had been making repairs in South Africa before I set off again to complete my world record. It wasn't until I left the safety of land and faced my first storm post-demasting that I realised how debilitating uncertainty, doubt, and fear can be. Surviving that demasting completely changed how I interacted with my boat and the weather. Every wave that crashed into the hull during the storm, and many after, would send my heart rate skyrocketing, my knuckles would whiten as I griped the rails while my mind reeled with questions – wondering if the next wave would break the boat.

As I sat huddled in the boat riding those liquid mountains, with the wind howling through the rigging, I came to the realisation that if I didn't get a handle on my fear I would lose the very thing that gives me drive. I would lose my passion for sailing. I love sailing and cannot think of a life without it, so giving in to my fear wasn't an option. I knew for me that the only way forward was through the fear. As I sat alone on my yacht in the Southern Ocean I reasoned things through. After that first storm, and then the next, I was able to overcome my fear, gain my confidence back, and push on.

Everyone copes with uncertainty, doubt, and fear in different ways. I was extremely grateful later that I'd been able to get back on that metaphorical horse and carry on – that sailing was still my future. As you devour the stories of these forty-six amazing women who wear their hearts on their sleeves and tell it like it is, hopefully you too will find your metaphorical horse and ride on into this amazing world of sailing, with all its ups and downs.

Lisa Blair, first woman to circumnavigate Antarctica solo.

Introduction

Enchanting, enticing, but also at times, terrifying; the sea beckons many of us. To others it is a 'necessary evil', something to endure as we seek to experience exotic locations, foreign cultures, or unusual wildlife encounters. Some are chasing a dream, others are following someone else's.

We are delighted to bring you a selection of true stories, written by women on (or in) the water. Each of our writers' experiences is unique but at the same time a common thread resonates – fear. While the things we fear may vary, the experience itself links us like an invisible thread.

As one of our writers points out, when we think of brave women on the water we think of round-the-world sailors such as Kay Cottee and Jessica Watson, or ocean racers like Wendy Tuck and Dee Caffari, or Lisa Blair the first woman to sail solo around Antarctica. These women take on challenges that many of us would never consider, even in our wildest dreams. In truth, however, every woman who casts off from the dock, or slips quietly below the water surface despite anxiety or deep-seated fear, is courageous in her own way.

While written by women, this topic is important for all genders. Throughout these pages you'll find women have opened their hearts and revealed their deepest fears. They've offered an insight into their world, how they react, and what they do to cope.

These stories are from around the globe and across the age spectrum. Given the diversity of our writers (and their locations), we've left the women's own voices and kept the localised spelling to highlight the flavour of our international contributions.

This collection hopes to highlight to those taking to the water for the first time, or struggling with ongoing fear, you are not alone.

We hope you draw some comfort and inspiration from these stories.

1

Butterflies

by Melissa Rout

Butterflies. It always starts with the butterflies. Hundreds. Tiny. Furiously beating their wings in unison. They live in my stomach and sometimes in my chest. I am filled with this pulsating relentless buzz in the pit of my gut. Not seasick. Not nauseous. I am not imagining this. I am scared. I have scared myself awake again.

I don't know what the time is. There is no moon. Laying in my cabin in the inky darkness, frozen in my fear, my mind and my ears have turned enemy. *How long have I been asleep? Is the anchor dragging? What is the tide doing now? Does that wind sound stronger than it did earlier? Has the wind changed direction? Is the anchor dragging? What about the other boats here in this hardly-protected anchorage? Are they staying put? Is the anchor dragging?*

Outside the boat a symphony is playing. Just the bass strings… the cellos and the double basses, their bows gently bouncing on the lowest notes. Then from above, the violas with a discord of wavering high-pitched whistling. Following this, a sound, not from the orchestra pit, not a musical sound at all. A commandment from the sea to respect and pay attention. The full, deep and gravelly growl of galvanised anchor chain dragging over rock and coral. This haunting sound then travelling up forty metres of the submerged chain, amplified through the fibreglass hull and played at full volume throughout the cabin, forced into my ears. This sound now the deep double bass under the bellowing wind that screams through the rigging, around the mast, and weaves in and out of every stanchion, sheet, and halyard.

I must move. Laying here wrapped in my fear and my salty sheets is not an option. With resignation, I make my way down the bed and reach for the door to the head. My hand stabs in the dark for the handle and I miss twice before grasping it, opening it and getting to my feet. The world around me is see-sawing and bucking and rolling, trying to topple me. The boat, like a bull pissed-off at being tethered, feels as though it is trying to break free from its anchor. I can almost see the look of defiance in the bull's eyes. The butterflies alter their course to starboard then port, swarming side-to-side in my stomach. I am not sick. This is fear. I fear all the things this night could bring.

Gripping the hand rails at the side of the companionway and cautiously climbing the stairs, I take a look outside. As my head clears the dodger a blast of confused air stabs at my face, pinches my ears, and makes me raise my shoulders, as though they will protect me, shelter me. Eyes squinting, I can make out another mast light nearby. *Or could it be a UFO? A UFO with a drunken alien pilot?* The movement of the glowing white beacon, hovering over fifteen metres up in the night sky, is violent and haphazard. Our mast light probably looks like that too. Masts forced into a macabre dance of sorts. There is some small comfort that we are not alone here. Fellow boater or inebriated alien.

Why I am such a drama queen? The instruments tell me the wind is only blowing fifteen knots, gusting to seventeen. Not the thirty-plus knots that I had convinced myself must be blowing. The anchor alarm has not gone off. Why? Because the anchor has not dragged. We are not being swept perilously towards the beach, the rocks, out to sea or on a collision course with another yacht or giant oil tanker. The anchor is doing its job. The tide has fallen but there are still three metres under the keel with only two more hours of tide to fall. Oh shit. *What was the tidal range again?* I know we had studied it thoroughly on the way here. Calculated it a dozen ways, each time coming up with agreeable numbers for us to safely anchor here without hitting the sea floor or swinging onto the beach or the rocks. But now I doubt the calculations. A cold sweat on my face, colder than the night air, now becomes hot. I do feel sick. I am not sick. I am not sick. I am afraid. I fear this night will drown me.

Back down below in the cabin I turn on a red light and rummage through the fridge for a thermos of ginger tea. My fingers search for the cold steel bottle and eventually recognise its smooth surface. Drinking straight from the bottle, just a few small sips. The taste is strong and sweet and feels good.

I contemplate looking over the tide charts again but assure myself I have already confirmed we are in enough water for the low tide and have enough chain out for the high tide. I stand staring at the cabin roof for a moment, my racing mind slowing from a sprint to a jog, then to a fast-paced walk, and finally I have my thoughts under control. I will sleep. The anchor alarm will alert us to any emergencies. I tell myself there won't be any. I will sleep. My eyes sting and then water. I rub them and turn out the light. Feeling my way back to bed, shivering as I pull the blankets up around my ears, I tell myself the wind sounds worse than it actually is. But the orchestra plays on and the bull is snorting and stamping his hooves. The butterflies swoop.

In my dream, I am at an indoor pool wearing a skimpy white bikini that I just know is going to be see-through when it gets wet. There are lanes of squad swimmers powering up and down the pool. I peer over the edge of the water and there are snakes. Twenty or so, large fat snakes swimming near the bottom of the pool. Their shapes are distorted and magnified by the movement of the water. Almost relieved at the sight of the snakes I decide there will be no swimming for me today. In the dressing rooms, with the sting of chlorine in my throat, I see three tiny snapping crocodiles on the concrete floor. I remove my thongs and kill them like they are insects.

And I'm awake again, the butterflies are doing loops and aerobatic stunts in my stomach. I become more aware of my surroundings. The orchestra and the bull and the butterflies. I reach for my phone to check the time. No service. SOS only. But it is 3 am. Two-and-a-half more hours before the sun's light will make everything better. At least I've had some sleep.

The wind continues to howl. There are too many creaks and groans from the boat to count, and no way to figure out which are harmless, and which may be something straining to its breaking point. Some integral piece of equipment that will give up tonight.

The oven door must have flown open as I can hear the unmistakable sound of my small roasting tin sliding across the cabin sole. I laugh out loud. A roasting dish. *What was I thinking? That we would be eating a civilised roast dinner out here in these lumpy waters? Really? Gravy? Wine in a glass? Actually, come to think of it, what was I thinking period? Why didn't I have safe and normal hobbies like my friends? Join the gym, coffee groups, book clubs, wine appreciation evenings, committees, learn a language, get a degree… What exactly was I trying to prove?* As I lay here now, tense and tired, I cannot imagine what drove me to this madness. *And people had tried to dissuade me, hadn't they? Did I listen?* Did I hell.

I have been sailing for at least ten years. Much longer if I count the times I sailed as a kid, terrified and sick, clinging to the rails for dear life and wishing I was anywhere but on the water. My father was unable to fathom that I had not inherited the salt gene from him. Now our family and friends cannot understand why we chose to live on a twelve-metre boat rather than enjoy the comforts on offer in our lovely home in the suburbs.

But hark, the call of the sea. I do have the salt gene after all. It just reared its watery presence later for me, and when it did come, it was strong and not to be ignored. So here I am. Scared and tired. Trying to reason with myself. Questioning my sanity. Submersing notions of regret. And knowing that, if nothing else, I am doing what I love. Answering the call of the sea. Madness or not. I silence the orchestra, untether the bull, and release the butterflies into the night.

Bio: Melissa Rout is fairly new to liveaboard cruising but has been quick to adopt the laidback lifestyle it affords. Currently cruising the East Coast of Queensland, Australia with her DH (Dear Heart) on their Catalina 380 *Surfer Rosa*, her favourite aspect of the cruising scene is the incredibly friendly and supportive fellow sailors she has met along the way. Melissa is, 'Making no plans, and sticking to them!'

2

10,800 Seconds

by Anna Whitaker

Ten thousand, eight hundred seconds: the exact number of seconds within three hours. More specifically, the three hours I spend on shift. Anytime we are on passage, that requires overnighting, we run shifts. Mine is twelve to three o'clock, once during the day, and once in the middle of the night.

Ten thousand, eight hundred seconds may not seem like a lot at first glance. On the day shift, they are three long, tedious hours that usually consist of changing sails, keeping an eye out, and listening to the same four playlists under the hot sun – wash, rinse, repeat. But that is during the day, with light and other people close at hand who are awake and alert. The worst-case scenario involving life or death during the day is if I fall off and can't swim. But I can, so that is not what terrifies me.

It's not the pleasant night shifts that terrify me, either. Those are easy to get a handle on. Calm seas and consistent winds and trimmed sails all contribute to that comfort. Once I shake off the grogginess from being woken up, and account for all the noises I hear – water washing against the hull, a line that needs to be tightened slapping against the mast, the rolling back and forth of a loose object inside the cabin – I tune them out and settle in with my book, occasionally performing the routine three-sixty glance around to make sure we're still on course and that we're not about to smash into anything unmarked on the navigation charts. I push away all my idle worries and let the time drag by.

No, it is not these conditions that choke me. These are hours that I use for reading, school, other productive things, or sometimes just staring at the sky and daydreaming. These are okay.

It is the chaotic night shift that increases my heartrate and thins my breathing. The three hours of being completely and totally alone, in the middle of the ocean with no sense of direction. The moon is new, providing no light, so that the water is pitch-black and endless, and my field of vision is non-existent. The waves swell up high and rock the boat to near-lethal degrees and saltwater washes over me in cold sprays. The winds roar and screech, relentless, snapping at the sails with tearing force. The ocean is chaotic and untameable, and I am paralyzed.

I grind my teeth against the nauseating heaves and sit stiff-backed in my seat. Every single nerve is on edge. I can't read or listen to music because I have to be ready at any given time to let fly a sail. My hands have a white-knuckle grip around my lifejacket, which is tethered to one of the jacklines, and now that my mind is on it, *these lifelines seem kind of flimsy, don't they?* A brave name for something that doesn't look like it could actually save my life.

Amidst the disarray and the internal panic, I realize I have to get up. I have to stand and do the three-sixty check. We're moving at nine knots, bordering on ten, and it feels like we're flying. The bow is tipping below the surface, but I have to get up. It takes me a minute to screw up all my courage, but I finally get to my feet on shaky legs, gripping whatever handholds are near. A quick look to the left, the front, the right, the back, so fast it barely even qualifies as a check. I drop back down to my seat, where I brace myself and try not to hold my breath. My fingernails dig into my palms sharply enough to break skin.

The noises are the worst. They jar harshly at my ears, each one screaming for my attention. Though I can identify them all and know that none are indicating anything wrong, I want to cry. I want to run inside and hide from everything caving in on me. Tonight, the ocean is a beast, and it is hungry.

My anxiety is cold and debilitating. I am wrapped in a cloak of fear. Terror crawls under my skin and rises in my chest and scratches at the back of my skull, threatening to break out in the form of scared tears. Dread manifests in the knowledge that everyone else onboard is asleep and that, should I trip and fall over these ill-named lifelines, no one will be coming to my aid. I will be dead before my feet even leave the deck.

When this realization comes to the forefront of my mind – as it does every night without fail – I force myself to take deep breaths. I'm not falling overboard. I'm tethered on, taking every safety measure I can.

Inhale, exhale. Nothing bad is going to happen. Inhale, exhale. Just a little while longer. Inhale. Exhale.

In the end, I can do nothing but wait it out. To make it more bearable, I repeat to myself that everything is fine, that we're on course and making good time. I check the clock and go by tens. Just get through the next ten minutes. Once those are up, I do another ten, and then another. Ten after ten after ten, and eventually, with a sigh of relief, I'm allowed to wake up the next watchman and get my hard-earned sleep.

I know that no matter how many night-shifts I do, I'm always going to stress at least a little. There's always going to be something that freaks me out and ratchets up my anxiety. But with each one, they get easier, bit by bit. I breathe a little deeper and my self-reassurances come quicker now. The ocean appears sentient, as if it's aware of us. Though it may be, it only gives this display of power to let us know that we are in its domain now. We are at its mercy, but it is nothing to be afraid of.

I count the stars, and I count the seconds. Only ten thousand, eight hundred to go.

Bio: By Anna Whitaker, a teenage girl sailing with her family of six around the globe!

www.youtube.com/sailingzatara

3

Paralysed in the Pacific

by Jill Carter

It's dusk on Day 16 of our passage from Galapagos to the Marquesas and we're counting down the nautical miles until we spy land once again. All around us, the vast and empty Pacific Ocean glistens in the setting sun as we reef down and prepare for another night out on the big blue. We're totally in sync and pumped to have more than two thirds of this passage now under our keel; excitedly we begin to plan our first excursions as we draw closer and closer to the Land of Men.

Night draws in and we settle into our evening routine. Paul, as always, takes the first watch and I head off for a few hours of contented sleep in readiness for my midnight to 0400 shift. We've learnt over the course of our world navigation which times work best with our individual body clocks and have set our routines to match.

I'm wrenched away from my dreams just after 2100 local time as Paul calls out for me to come to his assistance. The sea state has become much more boisterous and he's reefed in further to smooth out the violent jerking motion as we sail downwind. By the time I've jumped out of my bunk and scrambled into the cockpit, we've slowed from the 5-6 knots speed we were achieving to almost a dead stop – it's as if we've been captured by the long tentacles of a mythical kraken – we later surmise we'd been caught in a discarded purse-seine net. There's a thunderous 'BANG', we lose all steerage and immediately round up – it's got to be our rudder. There are a few shared moments of disbelief before we switch to automatic mode and deal with getting our sails down as quickly as possible. We pull in the headsail hastily, accompanied by the harsh beat of flailing canvas. We fight to furl our main, working hard to roll it down and into the boom. Once done, we sit… and the fear hits me with the power of an avalanche. We're out in the midst of the most isolated piece of water on the planet, we have no rudder, we cannot steer. A thousand doubts and worries are buzzing in my brain and I begin to shake. I look at Paul; he's shell-shocked too.

We sit awhile in scared, shared silence and try to pull ourselves together. We reach out for one another and sit, hugging tightly, as we process the enormity of the situation and to somehow form coherent thoughts.

Comforted by one another, the words start tumbling out as we voice our concerns and put together a disaster management plan. We're unhurt, we're floating, we're rudderless but we're safe. I grab the Sat phone and call our family at home in Western Australia, arranging for them to touch base with the Australian Maritime Safety Authority (AMSA); I get onto SailMail and log a position report. I even have the presence of mind to inform our insurers. Paul starts thinking steerage solutions and we determine that we'll try out the emergency tiller that we have onboard. We spend the remainder of the night wrapped in each other's arms, drawing comfort and strength in this intimate, yet horrifying moment of our lives.

We sleep fitfully. As dawn breaks, although we're tired from the lack of proper rest, we're fuelled by adrenalin and coffee as we pull apart our spare bunk and drag out all the components of the emergency steering system. It's a stainless steel six-piece kit with a three-foot squared rudder and a tiller arm, manufactured by Paul, and designed to get us out of short-term trouble. We put it together, piece by piece. It's difficult to bolt the bracket to our transom while fighting the very big and uncomfortable following sea, and we're praying that we don't lose a single, nut, screw or washer overboard as we do it. It's unbelievably hard and Paul, although clipped on, is washed off a couple of times during the process.

Two hours of intense teamwork later, it's assembled, and we are ready to test operating capabilities. It takes some time, and a few false starts, but we finally figure out by combining the grunt of the bow thruster while using the autopilot to turn what little rudder is left, we can at least set a course towards Nuku Hiva. We agree a plan to cover as many miles as we can each day, hoving-to at night to rest and to avoid overstressing the emergency rudder (affectionately now known as 'The Little Guy'). We know TLG doesn't have the strength to be engaged under sail and we resign ourselves to motoring our way across the Pacific to safety.

I struggle to manage the tiller and Paul becomes responsible for picking up my slack. AMSA message us through our SailMail system and request that we touch base with JRCC* Tahiti, which I immediately attend to. They enquire about our health and safety, our fuel supply, and our onboard provisions; I assure them that all is well, and we have sufficient food, water, and diesel. I agree to provide a twice daily position report and to inform them if we get into any difficulties. I contact the SailMail Association as I'm conscious that I'm going to be totally exceeding our weekly airtime allowance and am exceedingly grateful and relieved when they advise I can have unlimited access to the network. I'm managing communications with our family and friends, both through private messages and through a daily blog post. I'm maintaining contact with our insurers and I'm plotting position reports online. We're both playing to our strengths and working as a streamlined and cohesive team. It's only in the quiet of night, when we've switched off our engine for the day, that I afford myself the time to silently work through my fears. There's no alternative but to suck it up and stay strong right now. I know intuitively that Paul is wrestling these same demons in his head and I know that neither of us wish to breathe life into what we are manifesting internally.

We forge on. We're averaging around 80 nautical miles per day and are stoked that we are aided by the swell and the south east breeze to drift a further 5-10 nautical miles overnight. It's the same routine day-after-day, only lightened with the arrival of a red-footed booby who turns up and hitches a ride on Day 4 of our emergency. He's a distraction and a gift sent by the universe to provide some light relief with his antics. We're both appreciative that we've been blessed with his company and how he's able to divert our thoughts and pleased we can have a conversation about something other than our situation. We tick off the miles.

On Day 8 we're in new territory – we've been at sea for 24 consecutive days which is our longest time ever and surpasses our 3,400 nm Atlantic crossing in 2014. With less than 200 nm to go and obviously sensing land, our avian companion, who I've named Monsieur Rouge, decides it's time to leave. He tightrope-walks down the starboard rail, makes a strange clacking sound and flies away. We're alone again but there's no time to be apprehensive or for me to indulge in my suppressed feelings of dread. There's a huge swell that's agitated and angered the ocean and we're surfing off waves at up to 12.3 knots. It's scary and we're truly thankful for the way *Elevation*, our beautiful yacht, is handling the conditions. Paul is unbelievably stoic and I'm doing my best to match his emotionless state. I trust him implicitly and I know in that moment that we're invincible and we will get through this. We spend another uncomfortable night out in the open, sleeping only through sheer exhaustion. When we rise at dawn, we see that the weather gods have decided to throw everything at us and we spend our last day out dealing with squally winds, big seas, and a truly turbulent and confused Pacific. Even the channel between Ua Huka and Nuku Hiva delivers boisterous conditions but with the finish line in sight, we simply push through – nothing is going to stop us now.

How my heart soars as we round the Sentinelle De L'est; how my heart sings as we enter Baie De Taiohae and we set our anchor. All my suppressed fears, my anxiety, my concerns suddenly dissipate as if blown away on the breeze. I look at Paul, my soulmate and life partner, and see he's feeling just the same. We hug, we kiss, we give profuse thanks to both *Elevation* and 'The Little Guy'. This ordeal is over and both individually and together, we've conquered fear and adversity. I send one last message to JRCC advising of our safe arrival and joyously sign-off, 'All well onboard'.

*Joint Rescue Co-ordination Centre

Bio: I've been a full-time blue water cruiser since April 2010 and with my husband, Paul, have now amassed close to 50,000 nm under the keel of our 48' yacht, *Elevation.* Sailing became a retirement goal, and we were blessed to be able to farewell working life in our early 50s, casting off the lines and living the dream ever since. I hail from Fremantle and have been a member of the Fremantle Sailing Club since 2006. I'm a newbie to writing and in recent times I've been really enjoying blogging about both blue water adventures and each destination we've explored.

My blog is at:
http://www.sailblogs.com/member/elevation/

4

Panic! On The Caribbean Sea

by Lane McKelvey

Sitting on the saloon floor, darkness surrounded me as I gasped for air, my chest heaving between sobs. Staring out over the cockpit to the stern of the 40-foot Leopard catamaran, I watched the seas rise and fall beneath the boat; the wind gusting across her bow as we surfed down the front of the waves. My mind racing with thoughts so fast it was hard to catch any of them and hang on, *I can't do this. I am not cut out to be a sailor. I can't stay on this boat for the next three days. I'm going to die out here in the Caribbean Sea.*

***

It was a sunny day in Providenciales, Turks and Caicos Islands when my husband, Terence, and I stepped aboard our client's new-to-him sailing vessel. Finally, I was experiencing the 'other side' of our business and assisting on a delivery instead of sitting behind the computer running QuickBooks. Over the next few days, we carefully completed our pre-sail checks and inspections and provisioned for our passage to Grenada before we cleared out of customs.

We left the dock at sunrise to cross the Turks and Caicos bank with unobstructed views. Blue skies reflected on the crystal-clear water creating a stunning pool-blue hue to help guide us around coral heads, and successfully through the bank. *We are off to a good start!* I thought.

Night began to settle around us as we continued along our southbound course. My first true overnight passage! No longer was I skirting the Eastern Seaboard or motoring the Intracoastal Waterways of the United States, but I was offshore sailing between islands! The thought of being out on the water at night was suddenly as terrifying as it was exhilarating. Lights from Hispaniola twinkled against the dark sky and even darker water. I had the first watch before I would rouse Terence from his short-lived slumber for his turn at the helm. As midnight approached, I began singing louder and directing an imaginary choir to comfort myself in the darkness until, at last, it was my turn to sleep.

The next morning, I awoke to a problem: the starboard engine had stopped working sometime before dawn and we were limping along, aiming for San Juan, Puerto Rico, to refuel – the fuel gauge wasn't working so we thought maybe we hadn't filled her completely before we left – and we needed to conduct engine maintenance. With little wind to make use of the sails, we had to run on one engine, skirting the coast of Puerto Rico and praying our fuel supply would last.

Several hours later, not unlike the cult-classic sailing movie Captain Ron, we coasted into San Juan on fumes. Vowing to never quote Captain Ron while underway again, I tossed the lines to the customs agents who were waiting at the fuel dock for us, and rejoiced we made it to a complete stop right in front of the fuel pump.

After refuelling and grabbing a quick bite to eat at the restaurant adjoining the marina, we were motoring off into the sunset, past the old forts guarding the port entrance, with the starboard engine back in action. Taking the first watch as the sun set, I resumed our southerly direction. Within two hours of leaving San Juan the starboard engine began to struggle again. Running to the cabin below, I woke Terence from his sleep and brought him up to survey the instrument panel. Sure enough, the starboard engine was sputtering and trying hard to work to no avail. We were again down to one engine and between islands. Fearful of the night ahead, I regained control of the helm, so that Terence could snag a nap on the settee before his watch.

When I awoke the next morning, we were entering the Virgin Passage, picking our way through near-impossible-to-see lobster pots with our eyes set on Saint Croix, USVI, to track down a mechanic. A beautiful sunrise greeted us along our way and gave us hope that the engine would finally be fixed in Saint Croix. Just hours later we were preparing to anchor outside Christiansted when we discovered the anchor windlass was unable to operate properly. Attempting to anchor with one engine and a less-than-stellar windlass proved difficult but finally, after several attempts, we were securely in one place. Exhausted, we collapsed into sleep for the entire night.

Sunrise roused us from our sleep and Terence got to work attempting to bleed the fuel lines and change the filter. Some six hours into the venture, with a diesel mechanic talking him through the process via speakerphone, the starboard engine was fixed! We were, once again, ready to set off in our southerly direction with me taking the first watch. Setting the sails as we passed Buck Island, I was elated about moving forward and being under full-sail for the first time on the trip. Until night fell…

As dusk began to settle, marring the line between sea and sky, my stomach began to turn. Heat lightning flashed all around the boat and the lights of Saint Croix were slowly melting away behind us. A few cruise ships lit up the sky and water around them, giving me little comfort that we weren't going to be crushed under the several-thousand-ton passenger ships as they steamed along their routes. Dusk faded into darkness and I felt as if the expanse of sky was closing in around me. My heart began to race with pain radiating down my left arm and my vision grew spotty. Fear engulfed me; I thought I was suffering a heart attack at sea, at only 30 years old.

Tears burned hot in my eyes as the cascading negative thoughts filled my mind; I can't do this. I am not cut out to be a sailor. I can't stay on this boat for the next three days. I'm going to die in the Caribbean Sea. My breathing quickened until I was gasping for air as the wind changed direction and the swells started to build behind us. Stumbling down the steps to the cabin below I woke Terence from his short sleep; unable to speak any words, just cry and gasp for air. Taking me to the saloon he threw on his life vest and harness and clamored to the helm that I left on autopilot in my panic. Struggling to breathe, and with a tear-stained face, I watched him work masterfully at the helm from my safe place under the saloon table.

A few minutes later Terence reappeared before me, unbuckling my life vest and taking it off so I could breathe easier. My panic attack was beginning to subside, but I still couldn't get the words out to tell him what happened. Looking out over the swells I could feel the tears coming again and my breathing shortened. Grabbing my computer from the table, Terence opened it and told me to do what I do best in the difficult moments – write. Effortlessly, the words flowed from my fingers as I recounted the events of the evening leading up to my panic. Engaged in my writing everything else began to fade around me until, at last, I climbed up into the settee and collapsed into a deep sleep.

What seemed like mere moments after I fell asleep, I felt Terence shaking me, 'Get your vest, I need you to take the helm, so we can drop the sails. The winds have increased, and we are surfing down the waves.' I didn't have time for fear, my husband needed me. I could sense the urgency in the tone of his voice. If we wanted to reach Grenada and get home to see our little girl I needed to step up and go outside. Fumbling with my vest, I walked out and clipped myself in at the helm. Trying to breathe deeply to quell the panic I could feel rising, I pointed our bow into the wind as Terence scurried on deck to drop the main sail. My eyes darted between him and the instruments to ensure we were into the wind and unwavering. After what felt like forever, Terence came back to the helm and told me to take another nap before coming back out.

When my turn to take charge came again, daylight was breaking. The terror I felt the night before subsided and I felt ready to tackle the day and sail to Grenada. As if trying to tell me everything would be okay, dolphins danced alongside our bow, guiding us on our path.

A few days later we arrived safely into Prickly Bay, Grenada and grabbed a mooring ball on our first attempt. I could finally rest and prepare to fly home, feeling full of accomplishment, and prepared to tackle the next sailing adventure… in a few months.

Bio: Lane and her little family (a husband, daughter, and two dogs) sold their home and nearly everything they owned to move onto a 35-foot catamaran sailboat to enjoy a more simplistic life on the water. There was only one problem… Lane grew up in the middle of a cornfield in rural Ohio, USA and didn't have years of experience sailing that her husband did. A Midwestern girl by birth, the sea captured her heart and she ran after it. Two years later, Lane is excitedly looking forward to their fast approaching departure date when they loosen the lines for good and cast off from Charleston, South Carolina for the clear Caribbean Sea. Follow their adventure at www.caytolife.com

5

What's Our Plan?

by Brita Marie Siepker

March 2015 – Samaná, Dominican Republic.

We had sailed over to the Los Haitises National Park in the northeast of the Dominican Republic that afternoon, leaving our slip at Puerto Bahía Marina in Samaná for the two days we planned to be away. It was a glorious sail once the wind filled in after lunch, as it tends to do there. Close hauled, we were making five knots or so, straight across the Bahía de Samaná.

We came upon some fishermen, who were tending to their fishing nets in the water straight ahead of us. They shouted and motioned for us to steer around the nets, but we didn't have the wind angle to play with and we were certain our shallow draft (1.5 meters) and smooth full keel would skim over the tops of the nets. They pleaded with us, I reasoned with them, they pleaded more with us, I reasoned more with them, they crossed themselves, and we all held our breath as we sailed across their nets. In the end, we skirted across without a hitch, and they waved goodbye to us, relieved, after we'd passed.

The Dominican Republic is a poor country, the fishermen of Samaná among the poorest. They row rickety skiffs for hours a day from home to the coveted fishing spots, out at dawn and back home after dark. If they're lucky, they have a small, tattered sail to hoist that looks about as wind-worthy as an old bed sheet. If they're really lucky, they have an old beat-up outboard engine, which usually requires countless pulls to get started and stalls shortly thereafter. And yet, out to sea they go, day-in and day-out, to catch enough fish to feed their families. As we sailed by in our tank of an American sailboat with a Japanese diesel engine that never fails, we were humbled by their fortitude and courage, and baffled by the economics of it all. How can they possibly catch enough fish to feed their families and pay for their gasoline?

Leaving the fishermen behind in Bahía de Samaná, we pulled into Bahía de San Lorenzo an hour or two before sundown. I eagerly finished the last few pages of a sailing thriller I'd started the night before, just as we tucked in between the karsts*. We headed into the wind, threw the anchor and dinghied over to an inlet with cascading mangroves and a hiking trail at the end. We hadn't seen a soul since the fishermen in Bahía de Samaná, though there was a ranger station down the shore where we believed a ranger lived or worked.

We relished finally being alone at anchor; the solitude of the uninhabited islands and empty anchorages was one of the things we most loved about the Bahamas we'd just left behind, and, after a week at a marina in the Dominican Republic, it felt blissful to be back on the hook all alone. We toasted our sundowners and had a drink or two more over dinner. There are no streetlights in an uninhabited bay, and there is no atmospheric glow from skyscrapers at a seaside national park. There is a black sky full of stars, if the sky is clear of clouds. It wasn't. There is a moon crossing the horizon, showering land and water with its chalky light, if it's more than half full. It wasn't. It was dark, our anchor light at the top of the mast the only light for miles. It's hard to stay awake much past sundown in such a dark landscape, so, once we were done with dinner, we were headed to bed.

The sound of drums pierced the silent night. It sounded like three or four wooden bongos being beaten on the shore behind the karsts. For a brief second, I thought it must be an event organized by the ecotourism resort a few miles further into the bay – some sort of 'commune with the natives' evening that I imagine people who visit ecotourism resorts in developing countries would rave about to their friends back in the suburbs. But the drums dropped off quickly, and there were no other signs of ecotourists – no squeals of delight, no flashbulbs snapping selfies with the drum-beating natives. There was only silence – the silence we'd finally gotten accustomed to after a month in the Bahamas – a silence we never could have fathomed from our high-rise in Manhattan just months before. Drums followed by that silence was not something we were prepared for.

Two small outboard engines started up from the direction of the drums. Had the ecotourists taken a vow of silence and were now headed back to the resort? The outboards shifted into gear. They appeared to be zigzagging across the inlet, headed toward us slowly. Every minute or so, they would shift into neutral, and you could hear hurried, hushed voices – two or three men from the sounds of it.

I clutched for the captain. 'What's our plan?' The captain looked completely befuddled.

'What's our plan if these men try to board us? They probably have machetes!' I tried again.

The captain laughed and said, 'I'm going to lock myself down in the cabin and you're going to talk to them.'

'That's not a plan!' I screamed.

I sat as still as I could, trying to decipher their heading, distance and speed from the sound of their engines, straining my eyes to make out some sort of outline in the thick darkness, training my ears to make out the words they were murmuring. All that I could determine was that they were still coming closer. Images of being slashed up by a machete and sacrificed to the gods of the sea, or being hacked up and used for fishing bait, flashed before my eyes. The suspense novel I'd just finished was about a young woman kidnapped from her sailboat to harvest her heart for transplant. *Were organ sales legal in the Dominican Republic?*

'We need a plan!' I hissed.

'I'll bring you one of your golf clubs we've been carrying around for months – I'll bet it would be the only time this entire trip you ever use it,' the captain joked.

I hushed him, hoping the approaching men wouldn't hear him. The anchor light (which I usually love because its LED bulbs shine more brightly than any other boat in the anchorage) very clearly announced our presence. I implored the men not to look up, to pass by us without noticing. 'Por favor, por favor, por favor….' I pleaded under my breath.

They did pass by us, far enough away that we never caught a glimpse. When they were sufficiently clear, I crossed myself and shuffled off to bed. We had heard them hauling something over the sides – fishing nets we presume. Fishing is prohibited in the national park; the fishermen probably collect their nets under the shroud of darkness to avoid detection.

What's our plan the next time we're alone at anchor and hear a boat coming at us? Never again to read a suspense novel about sailing. And lock myself in the cabin before the captain does.

*Karsts: Landscape underlain by limestone which has been eroded by dissolution, producing ridges, towers, fissures, sinkholes and other characteristic landforms.

Bio: Brita Siepker learned to sail at the Manhattan Yacht Club in New York. She has been cruising full time since January 2015 and is currently circumnavigating with the World Arc 2018/2019. You can follow her adventures at www.lifeiswater.com

6

Holding on and Untied

by Judith Maizey

Hundreds of pieces of glass lay scattered on the floor. Not shards of glass but lots of little glass briquettes, much like little bits of Lego – except these blocks were not pretty coloured and would never fit neatly together to make buildings, planes, or even little ships like Lego.

This pile of glass had been two windows on the starboard side of our 20-tonne, trawler-style boat, but was the least of our problems at the time.

Two days prior, on the Friday and with my husband and a friend aboard, we left our Gold Coast marina in near perfect weather conditions to anchor up in Moreton Bay to relax, put the crab pots out and, if we were lucky, catch some fish for dinner.

No fish were caught, but we did score two legal-size male mud crabs that were cooked and lavishly spread on fresh bread rolls with a little pepper, salt, and lemon juice for lunch one day.

With several commitments on Monday, coming back on Sunday afternoon in 20 knot winds was not ideal, but we had no choice.

Certainly, the prospect of tying up our 15-metre boat in a pen alongside another similar-sized vessel was not one I was looking forward to.

Like a lot of marinas, there was not a lot of room to manoeuvre between the rows in our marina and we only had about two metres of leeway between the boats in our pen. But we had a bow thruster and although we'd owned the boat only four months, my husband was confident everything would be fine.

As a relative newcomer to boating, I was not so confident – but I was not the skipper and my husband and a mate had brought the vessel back to the Gold Coast from Melbourne through horrific, four-metre seas in Bass Strait, whereas I had not.

So, with three fenders in place and ropes at the ready on our starboard side for a bow-in tie-up, my husband started the process of gingerly lining up our boat.

A boatie living in the marina had come onto our jetty to help tie up and catch a rope, this was not going to be easy considering gusts of wind were blowing our boat every which way.

With my heart racing, I tossed the bow line and it was quickly caught, but instead of tying the rope off around a cleat, the catcher opted to just hold on to it and that's when things went pear-shaped very quickly.

A bullet of wind pushed our boat to port and the rope-catcher, fearing he was going to be dragged into the water by our boat, let the rope go.

Big mistake. HUGE.

What was then probably only a matter of minutes, but which seemed like hours, my husband tried desperately to bring our vessel back under control while I got someone, anyone, to secure her lines.

Ricocheting off the bowsprit of the other boat in our pen, we hit the anchor of a yacht in the next pen.

As more boaties popped their heads up on deck in nearby boats, to come and help and/or watch, a split-second decision was made by someone that it would be better or easier to tie up our tormented vessel in a pen at the end of the row than in our designated one.

With instructions coming loud and fast from people on the pontoon and with me relaying them to my husband at the helm as he could not hear them over the roar of the winds, our pride and joy moved slowly without incident to the end of the arm.

More lines were tossed, caught and looped quickly around cleats and, much to my relief and that of my friend, we were soon tied up and the engines shut down.

Someone kindly said I appeared quite calm through the whole horrific incident. Little did they realise how terrified I was and how out of control everything had appeared to me.

Several people said to my husband, 'There, but for the grace of God, go I'. I think it was said to make him feel better, but I suspect at the time it didn't.

An audit of the physical damage to our boat revealed two smashed windows in our saloon from hitting the bowsprit, bent stainless steel railings, and warping along the starboard side. Two other boats also received damage, but relatively minor in the scheme of things.

Fortunately, no-one was hurt, and insurance covered the boat damage, but the injury to my confidence was like that of the damage to our boat. Big. HUGE.

With our vessel on the hardstand for months undergoing repair, I wondered if I would ever get the courage and confidence to step foot on her again.

But like falling off a horse, I did get back on her when she eventually went back in the water and now truly love my cruising lifestyle, the people I have met along the way and the places I have been.

It did, however, take me nearly four years to honestly say that I'm no longer gripped by fear when we tie up in a marina now.

A little anxious maybe, but not fearful – although my heart does still race if someone I don't know offers to take our lines.

If they knew what I had been through, I'm sure they'd understand why I sometimes wail like a banshee for them to use the cleat, tie us off, and not stand there casually holding a rope by hand – a rope that's attached to a boat weighing 20 tonnes!

Bio: Bon vivant, wanderer and writer. Mother, wife and friend. A student of life, always learning. Semi-retired after more than 30 years as a journalist and public relations specialist.

7

Wild Wind on Anchor

by Rachel Alford-Evans

Wind can be an interesting mistress. She is obviously a gentle friend when she is kindly and consistently flowing at 15 knots from the southwest quarter, and you are on a happy beam reach under full sail and blue skies. Then, as it often happens in New Zealand, she will change temper like a menopausal woman and morph into a wild, ugly, ten-headed demon, harshly gusting to 50 knots. This wild side of the wind can become both a battle and an exercise in perseverance when sailing, and a beast to face when it's pitch black, pouring with icy rain, and you are on anchor in an unfamiliar harbour.

We had recently joined the ranks of 'live aboards' at the tail end of autumn after a strenuous summer of house renovations that made it impossible to leave earlier. Fellow sailors suggested we could make our first port of call the Mahurangi Harbour. It seemed to us a happy kind of a place to ease our way into our new way of life so off we went. Everything was peachy for the first few days, just as imagined. The wintery front building and heading our way looked very manageable compared to the 60-knot side on blasts we'd just experienced in the marina. We did, however, struggle to make a decision about where to anchor. All of the most protected spots in the harbour were either too shallow or taken up with moorings. After some discussion we opted for wind exposure but good swell shelter and mud holding in the inner harbour near Grants Island. This seemed preferable to the very unpleasant big roll coming into Sullivan's Bay. The forecast overnight was for a manageable 20 knots. We settled in comfortably, had dinner and were chilling out when I did my standard end-of-day check of the weather forecast. It had changed completely and was now predicted to be 35 knots, gusting 50-knot plus. Cool, thanks for that MetService, did you really not know that at your scheduled forecast time two hours ago?

I felt let down, as by that time it was dark and raining, with the wind starting to rise. Such combined factors made the prospect of change more hazardous, it was better to stay put and weather it. I knew immediately that I would not be sleeping even if I was lying down, so I reasoned with my husband (who looked exhausted) that in the past I was the night owl and would stay up for the first four-hour watch.

Night thoughts come unbidden, like waves over your bow as it plunges again-and-again into a swirling dark grey, short, choppy sea. They whirl around like a tidal eddy; *Have we anchored well? Will we hold where we are? Why didn't the wind funnel down the valley like that when we anchored in the daylight? How far are we going to swing? Have we got enough warp out? Have we got too much warp out and will we take out those other boats? How well anchored are our neighbours, and will they drag into us? We have nobody nearby to help if something does happen.*

The howling shriek and shudder of the rigging as your floating home suddenly and violently pitches to the side does nothing to ease those thoughts and worries. Fear grips its little fists around your ever-cooling heart. Your children lying anxiously in their berths do nothing to ease the worry as they beat their little butterfly wings of emotions raggedly against what's left of your ease. That's the thing with sister wind isn't it, you have no say and no control over what she chooses to do.

'Sleep my little one sleep, fond vigil I keep, lie warm in your nest, by moonbeams caressed. When the dawn tints the sky, God will wake you and I.'

As I sang this comforting family lullaby I fervently hoped that we would greet the new dawn in a peaceful manner and would all actually manage to get some sleep before dawn.

My son laughed saying, 'Mum this song is very appropriate for tonight, you are actually standing vigil'. And so I was. In fact, I was on high alert to start off with and had that cabin completely organised. Everyone's life jackets were immediately to hand right by the hatch and I was fully dressed in my overalls, boots, and wet weather jacket. *After all the rule is put your own gas mask on first, right?* I had a plan to have the engine on and be able to be outside in less than 30 seconds if anything untoward started happening. There are many things you can't plan for, but that small plan gave me focus. I felt slightly more in control knowing I could at least start navigating the unknown should it arise. I needed to be responsible and face this situation with confidence for a change, to feel I could be the one making good decisions for my family and our home.

It was a surreal and lonely experience sitting in a small cold cabin with red glowing LED switchboard lights and sleeping family for company. Yet despite the heavy rushing squalls, bucking tidal pull, and singing rigging, I felt the sailors knot between my shoulder blades loosening as the night wore on. We felt good in the water and were weathering the situation well; our anchor was holding us in place. I slowly felt more settled hearing the rush of the gusts and recognising how we were responding in the situation. As I had hoped, by pushing myself to take charge, I had found somewhat of a sense of peace and rhythm in the situation. The squalls were no less intense, yet they had an underlying sense of breathing. Not regular but recognised and welcomed by the tide and body of water that lay beneath me.

Gradually I became tired and cold, moving around the small circuit of wiping windows and peeking through the makeshift and easily moveable main hatch door to check the outside light markers and the instrument panel. It seems I'm not the night owl I once was, and the deliciously tempting safety net of sleep was closing around me as I watched the children in their slumber. I managed to hold out as long as possible until my husband awoke. Thankfully that was right on the three-and-a-half-hour mark just as I was starting to drift on the raft of sleep. It felt good being able to pass on helpful information, including that we were sitting well now the low tide had passed. I pointed out what my 'landmarks' were and climbed into the v-berth saying, 'If you go outside make sure you have your lifejacket on because I'm about to sleep like a rock.' And I did, solidly without qualm for the next three-and-a-half hours until my next watch. It was bliss.

As a woman over 45 I have sometimes wondered at the wisdom of choosing now to live aboard a small yacht with my husband of 14 years and two children in their early teens. Being stuck in a confined space with 'nowhere' yet 'everywhere' to go is a strange feeling. Add unpredictable weather and my inexperience into the mix and things can occasionally get a bit heady. 'Feel the fear and do it anyway' was the catch phrase of a self-help book I tried to read many years ago. The title is really the only thing that stuck with me, but that has been enough. I don't wait for fear to go away before I do what I want or need to do. I feel it, struggle with it, embrace it, and go.

More than anything the process of sailing off into a sea of unknown situations has pushed me to be active in facing fears and voicing my intuitions. Every day aboard has a heightened sense of immediacy and little room for complacent navel gazing. I love the glorious crazy aliveness I have experienced being so present with my family, the wind, the ocean, and myself.

Bio: Exploring coastal New Zealand is where you'll find Rachel. She is passionate about lifelong learning, adventure, sustainability, family, food, fine photography, and the sea.
You can find her on Facebook @svenasailing
Instagram storieswithoutwords.nz
Or on the Web www.storieswithoutwords.nz

8

Suddenly Racing

by Ashleigh Douglas

As a novice sailor, the most alarming part for me has been adjusting to the movement of the boat while under sail. Our first boat was only 27 feet and not overly heavy in the water, so a good gust of wind would knock her about quite a bit. We owned *Serenity* for only twelve months before upgrading and every time we would take her out on the lake I'd seat myself on one side of the cockpit with my feet braced against the opposite seat and my hand gripping the nearest stanchion rail in preparation for what was to come.

On one occasion, we set off from our mooring with all sails flying. The wind was about 15 knots that day and we were speeding across the lake. A yacht race was in full swing, starting in Belmont and looping a marker in the middle of the lake. We had the genoa and the full mainsail out on the starboard side as we crossed in front of the Swansea Channel opening. As we ducked and weaved between several boats who were on their return trip, a gust swept through from the south east tipping the whole boat on its side. The toe rail was in the water, the bottom of the genoa was brushing the waves and Brett was standing on the side of the cockpit with both hands on the steering wheel and a huge grin on his face.

I'd never felt so scared in my life. My feet were pushing against the other seat so hard that they started to hurt, my hand gripping the stanchion rail had turned white from the force and a volley of involuntary squeals and sounds escaped my lips as I struggled to hold on. We tipped and swayed with the passing gusts, attempting to turn ourselves out of the wind's forceful grasp and unfortunately into the direct path of one of the racing yachts. I looked at the angry, horrified faces on the racing yacht as they hurriedly pulled on ropes and swung away from us, swearing at us as they did. I yelled a massive, 'SOOOORRRRYY!' into the growing gap between our boat and theirs as they tacked away.

After what felt like ten minutes, the wind finally dropped, and the boat sprung upright. The boys hurried to furl in the genoa as I struggled to regain my composure. Reece had told me several times that, 'boats want to be upright,' and this experience taught me that was true. Once the wind was gone, the boat bobbed back up like a cork as if nothing had ever happened.

Six months later, on our next boat, a 40-foot monohull, we had a similar thing happen – again in the lake.

We had decided to sail around Pulbah Island – the first time we'd done so – on a fairly blustery day. As we sailed around the north side of the island, the wind was roughly at 20 degrees to the bow so we managed to get around that side without having to tack at all. The island blocked the wind so we just casually cruised until we rounded the other side and were hit by the full force of 20 knots so suddenly and completely on the beam that the entire boat heeled over until the mast was at a 15-degree angle to the water. Another six months of experience meant that Reece was better at coping this time. He changed position, so he was standing on the side of the cockpit and steered his way out of the wind with me whooping and hollering the whole time. For quite a while, after this occasion, I was hesitant to sail any time the forecast was more than 15 knots.

While we haven't had another one of these incidents happen in the last 18 months, I feel a bit more confident in dealing with it now that I've been sailing for nearly three years and completed a few trips of ocean sailing from Lake Macquarie to the Hawkesbury. I'm sure my confidence will continue to increase as my sailing experience does.

Bio: I'm a part time sailor hoping to become a full-time traveller and sailing extraordinaire. I love writing about everything and also run a YouTube vlog about my boating experiences, called *Sailing Barnaby*. www.sailingbarnaby.com

9

My Nemesis

by Lyn O'Dwyer

I was chucking a full-on tanty.

I was prepared to do just about anything on our boat, but I was flatly refusing this time. I could not do it.

Through my tears, I looked longingly at the yachts merrily tucked up along the strip of tavernas around the water's edge. We'd just come from there. Our mooring had broken almost as soon as we tied up. Now it was blowing 25-30 knots and we were circling around the choppy bay while I argued with my husband, Brian.

I wasn't normally such a wimp. I have a certain low level of anxiety that hums through me when it comes to our cruising life. From worrying about finances and possibly spending my retirement in a cardboard box, to afternoon meltemis* belting us, to always keeping an eye out for our sea dog's safety. I often feel anxiety but not gut-wrenching fear. We'd already weathered a 40 knot spume-throwing-blast off Datça and in my younger years I'd raced keel boats across the heaving waves of Bass Strait. Those things hadn't filled me with the same dread as now, as I refused to do what needed to be done that day in Cokertme Bay.

My melt down was over a stern tie-up.

I'm not talking about a nice, back-in-to-a-wide-jetty, with a friendly local or marina staff member to take your lines. I'm talking about a drop-your-anchor, jump overboard, swim like crazy, scramble up rocks and execute the perfect bowline tie up, while your boat is wildly swinging in cross winds and threatening to take out your neighbours – type of tie-up. I had watched enviously as gullets and mega yachts had come into anchorages and their crew shot ashore in high-speed inflatables and secured the boats in five minutes flat.

Ever since we'd arrived in Turkey I'd found ways to avoid having to do a stern tie-up. Despite my foot stomping and dramatics, the time had come when I had no choice. The anchorage was almost full. There were no more moorings available for a yacht our size. It was blowing a gale.

I managed to pull myself together by focusing on preparation. This miraculously did not include an alcoholic drink. I attached all the fenders and lugged the long lines down to the stern of the boat. I put my silicon shoes and flippers where I could easily grab them. I gave the OK to Brian and we made our way into the shore.

Our boat, *Astarte*, is a beautiful 53-foot Wharram Pahi catamaran. She is a dream to sail and has enough deck space to host a barn dance, but she does not spin on a dime like modern cats and monohulls. She has to be coaxed. The first challenge was manoeuvring her into a gap between two boats where the shore had some likely looking rocks to tie to. The wind kept catching her bow and pushing her down onto one of the boats. We had room, but it was a bit dicey in the conditions.

Next, I had to drop the anchor. I had no idea when to start dropping the anchor or how much chain to let out. Too little and the lines wouldn't reach. Too much and we might end up on the rocks. I let out the chain, calculating approximately how much I thought we needed and we were in position.

I quickly put on the flippers and jumped overboard with the first line in my hand. I had to swim one-handed as quickly as possible to the shore. Meanwhile, the wind had taken *Astarte* again and the line was being ripped out of my hand. I kicked as hard as I could while Brian worked the engines. I thought we'd hit the boat downwind of us for sure.

Once I made it to the rocks, I couldn't climb up them because of the flippers and I couldn't get one of them off. I was flapping around like a dying fish. Finally, I scrambled past about a hundred sea urchins and up the rocks, which tore the arse out of my bathers and me, and wrapped the line around a sturdy rock. I didn't have enough slack to secure it and *Astarte* was nudging up to our neighbours again. More engine manoeuvring and some yelling later I had enough rope to tie up. Despite tying them hundreds, if not thousands, of times I suddenly could not tie a bowline. By now, I wasn't panicking but I was crying.

Inspiration struck. The line was tied. Brian pulled forward on the anchor and we were safe and the people on boats around us sighed with relief. In retrospect, they were never really in danger, but I didn't have that perspective at the time. I still had to swim back to the boat and collect the second line. This time it was easier without so much tension (on the rope or between the spouses) and we were secured.

I dragged myself back on the boat. It was the day before my 55th birthday and my lack of fitness showed. I was exhausted. I did manage to raise a glass of wine to my lips.

I have learned a lot about stern tie-ups since then. I have refined my technique and when there is no wind we manage to do them neatly and with minimum fuss. However, I have also battled cross-winds, and our seemingly wilful boat, and taken forever to tie up. I'm getting better, but I haven't completely conquered my fear. I still get that sinking feeling when the cruising guide book says, 'Take a long line to shore.'

I know that many women who sail have faced enormous challenges and hardships and faced terrifying experiences and come out the other side. I admire them all.

My courageous act is to admit that stern tie-ups are my nemesis.

*Strong, dry north winds of the Aegean Sea.

Bio: Lyn and her husband chartered yachts around the world before buying their own to sail the Queensland coast for a year. They recently bought a Wharram Pahi 53 in Greece and are currently sailing around Turkey and Greece with their dog, Scooter. Lyn does a bit of writing on the side.

10

Our Earth Provides

by Sheena Jeffers

Thomas Merton wrote, 'It is true that we are called to create a better world. But we are first of all called to a more immediate and exalted task: that of creating our own lives.'

When I first started to wrap my head around this 'sailing life', I struggled. I bubbled over with hesitations, questions, and concerns.

How do I make money? I can't just leave. What about insurances? What about my career? What about my future? What will I do when the money runs out? How will I have food and stable shelter and create a life and, basically, survive? What if my relationship, when forced to bob lifelessly on waves in the middle of the ocean, fails?

Fear consumed me. I was a scarecrow of straw stapled to a wooden stand, mentally and emotionally landlocked and pecked at.

Then one day, a sailor said to me while casually popping pistachio shells from the nut, 'You need to stop worrying. Work will appear. Food will appear. Friends will appear. Purpose will appear.'

Was I under the impression that I was in full control of all things (work, food, friends, purpose) on land? Had I bought and swallowed the idea that the only way to exist is to be an employee for an employer and buy my food from available stores, buy my insurances and repeat my days?

I started to see my fears stemmed from lack of trust in the world around me and in nature. Deep-rooted trust issues. But I couldn't lie down in the office of a therapist with my feet up and say, 'I have been so steeped in commercialization, societal expectations, and modern comforts that I seriously don't trust nature.'

I never assume that someone will 'take care' of me or 'handle things' for me. That was always my job, my responsibility. But in sailing, 'taking care' and 'handling things' are packaged differently.

Society taught me to fear, and fear greatly. The world of people convinced me that I somehow have control of this thing called life as long as I stay stable, in line, do what I'm told, pay my bills, buy the insurances, and wait.

But what was I waiting on?

If you ask Geico (car insurance), I was waiting on a possible flood, fire, or horrific car accident. If you ask my health insurance, I was waiting on a pestering cold, chronic condition or a heart-wrenching diagnosis. If you ask my career, I was waiting for an employer to recognize my potential and talents and have the financial capability to promote me. If you ask my love life, I was waiting for a marriage proposal. If you ask my school loans, they're just waiting for me to pay them (while secretly celebrating that I can't pay them all off at once), and if you ask my mortgage, it feels the same way as my school loans.

All of this waiting… and for what?

As I started to put the pieces together, I stumbled upon a Bible verse one morning:

"Therefore, I tell you, do not worry about your life, what you will eat or drink; or about your body, what you will wear. Is not life more than food, and the body more than clothes? Look at the birds of the air; they do not sow or reap or store away in barns, and yet your heavenly Father feeds them. Are you not much more valuable than they? Can any one of you by worrying add a single hour to your life?" [Matthew 6:25-34]

It hit me: I needed to trust in powers larger than myself and any human-created system, insurance policy, or plan. ASAP.

I packed my bags, left my fear trembling on the dock, and sailed away.

I pour myself a cup of coffee and walk outside to water our plants. Ten miles offshore, surrounded by the ebbs and flows of water splashing against the bottom of the boat, we move with the sway of the swell. I water our plants. Curled, mature tomato leaves hiding a tomato so vibrantly red and pregnant with vitality, it's about to drop; bright basil, refreshing mint, and the infant beginnings of squash, cucumbers and lettuce.

I sit down with my cup of coffee and listen, deeply, as the wind twists through our sea glass wind chime; the high-pitch clinks creating an unpredictable rhythm. I have learned to sink into nature's unpredictability.

I had never before noticed nature's keen intuition. Her impeccable way of noticing what everything and everyone needs. Her intentions: providing for, rocking, supplying, serving, re-grouping, re-claiming, healing itself and everyone nearest to it. I had never felt her pulse and breath as it expands and contracts. I had never been tossed by nature's playful, stubborn, and tricky ways; an ocean current desires, with gusto, to push you one way while the wind decides to blow another, all while the moon is commanding the tide to abide. Opera singers trying to out sing each other with supported and powerful breath.

Since my life change (and mindset change), I witness plentiful fish, bodies full of hearty meat, being offered up from the ocean. This meat sustains us, fuels us, provides nourishment for us.

Sunrises awaken our cells, tingling their way into motivation for the day. Sunsets make heavy our eyelids. These cycles bookend our days.

Work pulls on creative uniforms and appears in different streams as we monetize our blog, land freelance writing contracts, offer donation-based yoga and imagine daily new, innovative streams of income.

I soak in new ways to experience friendships and family.

I experience a freedom I never thought possible to achieve. A freedom where my days are open, unscheduled, claimed for by only myself, and moved in unanticipated directions. I am living from my imagination instead of my fear, and I wake up every day whispering, 'Thank you.'

I left the stability and structure of a full-time job and threw myself into a whirlwind of having to trust everything and everyone around me. It wasn't an easy transition and it requires of me to conjure up different parts of myself, unknown to me before. It demands of me to have confidence in myself and not allow others to bring me down or convince me that I'm not worthy.

I never expected these lessons to come from nature.

But I now recall my last appointment with my functional medicine doctor. I sat nerve-wracked, feet anxiously dangling from her table. She looked up from the note she just marked on my chart: Leaving to travel the world by water. She said, 'You become what surrounds you. You're becoming water full of waves.'

This phrase repeats itself to me. How lovely it has been to become a body of water – fluid, flexible, ever-changing, persistent, and self-sustaining. How strong it is to live full of waves – transitive, powerful, influential, responsive.

If there is anything I've learned from the nature that now surrounds me and fills me, it is that there is a big, beautiful world out there that wants to love us, care for us, share with us, and test us. Most importantly, nature doesn't work from a place of fear, so I, imitating her, no longer allow fear to choke me.

Bio: Sheena is a freelance writer from Richmond, Virginia who had never sailed a day in her life before. She and her boyfriend sold their home in order to purchase and pay off their Catana 431, *Seas Life.* In 2017, they tossed off the dock lines from Norfolk, Virginia and started making their way through the Caribbean with no plans other than to "Seas Life." The sailing couple, currently anchored in Cartagena, Colombia, has been featured on Today.com and Distinction Magazine, but spend most of their time figuring out the perfect time to remove cookies from their solar oven.

To follow their adventure logs:
www.seaslifeforgood.com or @seaslifeforgood on Instagram.
To follow their YouTube videos:
https://www.youtube.com/c/SeasLifeforGood.

11

Adopt Your Fear

by Stefania Capece Lachini

When I was a little girl I was afraid of the dark. I guess most little girls are. I used to call my dad if I woke up in the middle of the night because I knew that once he was in the room he would turn on the light and talk to me. That was enough to blow the fear away most of the time. Some other times I wouldn't let him go away, crying in anticipation of what was to come once the darkness came back.

One of those nights I asked him if he was ever afraid. My dad to me was (and still is) absolutely perfect and I couldn't think of him being scared of anything. He told me that he had been scared plenty of times in his life. Then he revealed his trick to me. He said that everything that scared him most he would do as soon as possible, because once you do it, it doesn't scare you anymore.

It didn't make any sense to me at the time, but I trusted him, and I tried to figure out ways to use his technique.

One of the things I was afraid of in the dark was being sucked down by a monster under my bed, so one night I tried to sleep under the bed myself. It didn't work well, because at one point I woke, and I tried to sit up, banging my head. It was partly successful: being able to fall asleep under there was a pretty big deal for me. Then one night it hit me. I always wanted a puppy, so I decided to adopt the monster and from that moment on I wasn't afraid anymore. The scary monster became an adorable weird-looking pet living under my bed to keep me company.

Growing up, this approach to fear wasn't always safe, but it allowed me to live a lot of incredible experiences. I was afraid of drowning, so I got my scuba diving certificate. I was afraid of heights, so I hiked as many mountains as I could. I was afraid of being alone, so I moved out to the country on my own. I was afraid of silences, so I started travelling solo and I found people to talk to on every corner… and so on.

Then something snapped. I don't know what it was. Maybe a new-found stability. Maybe hearing everyday news of women being abused or killed for living freely. Maybe I just got lazy. I became accustomed to safe environments. I started telling myself that being afraid wasn't a bad thing. That fears make us aware of what could be dangerous. It is an evolutionary superpower.

Of course, that is true, but what is an even more important evolutionary superpower is our ability to overcome fear. The ability to adopt the monster who lives under the bed.

One day, not so long ago, I realized that it had been more than five years since the last time I travelled solo. I realized it after someone I know asked me about Scotland. I had planned a trip to Scotland and invited basically everyone I knew to join me, nobody did, so I didn't go. I didn't want to go alone. I was afraid it could be dangerous. I was afraid I'd feel lonely. I was afraid I wouldn't have anyone to talk to. It only took it a few years of distraction and fear took me back to the starting line.

That shocked me.

I thought about it a lot and I tried to figure out a way to use my dad's technique. I found online a post about some people needing crew for a sailing delivery from one side of my country to the other. It was a chance to go sailing again, but most importantly it was an unfamiliar environment.

Of course, I took every precaution I could, but the challenge of trusting strangers was what I needed most.

I was also very scared of getting seasick. I never had been before, but I cannot imagine anything worse, especially when you have to sail for several hours. On this delivery, we would need to do a minimum of 20 hours at the time, in the cold, early-spring weather.

The day before leaving I was trembling in anticipation. We arrived at the boat, slept in it the first night and the morning of the departure I woke up happy as a child.

Every hour I spent at sea was pure joy. The nights were particularly magic, I could barely sleep. I needed to see the moon on the sea, to look at her go all through the night sky to set at the exact same time the sun would rise on the opposite side.

One night, after a whole day without wind, we spent several hours working our sails and route to use the few knots there were. It was a constant adjustment. And then the gods helped our endeavours and the ship started swooshing in the water. I always thought that the best thing about sailing is that moment when you turn off the engine and all you can hear is the wind on the sails and the sea on the hull. I breathed the purest air my lungs could know. Filled with freedom, self-accomplishment and new found confidence. I was at sea, with new friends, doing something I loved. I wasn't alone. I wasn't afraid. My ears and eyes filled with wonder. I started smiling and then, on the far side of my right eye, a dolphin jumped out of the water.

When I came back home I was changed. I grew uneasy at my job and my life. I realized that in the act of being safe I had crushed my dreams. It was going to be a challenge, but I needed to start living strongly. I decided to take a break from my work and find something I was really passionate about and focus on that. I wanted to keep sailing and travel as much as I could. Who knows, maybe one day I'll sail around the world!

I now take risks every now and then, because most of the time it's worth it. I don't want to be afraid just because I'm a woman. I need to believe that the world can change. And if it doesn't I need to believe that I can live in it being free nonetheless.

If one day, travelling around, you see a girl with an under-the-bed-monster sitting by her side, that's me: *I'm afraid, but it's ok*!

12

Navigating Fear

by Lanise Edwards

I've always attributed 'bravery' to those who climb mountains, sail oceans single-handed in treacherous seas, or risk their own lives to save another without thought of self. I still consider these acts as immensely 'brave'. However, I've learnt that there is another type of 'bravery' and with it comes paralysing fear. Fear held me tight, invading my mind, locking me in a frozen place. In hindsight it was not illogical. At one time, fear made me feel totally ashamed, an absolute failure. Between 2012 and 2014 a series of tragedies occurred within my small family that shook me to my core and changed my mindset, creating a horrendous fear of losing anyone I loved.

On September 19, 2013, our only child, our daughter, was killed in a car accident on the Pacific Highway in New South Wales, Australia. Alex had just turned 23 years old. A year before this, almost to the day, my husband had experienced a terrible boating accident that almost took his life and left him with horrific injuries. We thought we had narrowly escaped the worst life had to inflict after my husband's accident, we had not. Nine months after we lost our precious daughter, my husband became extremely ill and again 'life' threatened to take him. I was done being hopeful. Previously I felt a naive faith in the universe to look after those I loved. Life had now turned savage, inflicting suffering and untimely death at any given moment. We were alone in this torment. This was the reality I now lived…

We scrambled to search for some sanity, some meaning to our lives. So much of life had been torn away from us and our daughter. Our conclusion was to return to the sea, a place we were familiar with. In previous decades we had sailed extensively. Selling up our home and most of our possessions was followed by my resignation from secure employment. I jumped in headlong and without much thought about fear. 'Fear' was about to engulf me in a manner I had never felt before.

We were feeling very vulnerable when we found *SV Easter Rose. Easter Rose* felt welcoming and kind; a type of refuge. It was as if she knew the sad fragility of her new owners. Ivy, our old Labrador dog, adjusted slowly to living aboard a 40-foot yacht after only ever living on land. We prepared *Easter Rose* as best we could for our journey north. At the same time a strange freeze was settling over me, I didn't understand what it was.

The plan: To sail north from Coffs Harbour towards our daughter's birth place in Cairns. We motored out of the marina and I was flooded by fear. Stupid, stupid fear; fear of sinking, fear of my husband falling over board! I didn't remember feeling this way previously and I tried to contain it as we headed to the Clarence River. A nasty bar crossing ensued and again I was convinced someone would die. By now I had made a few sailing friends, some online and some face to face… many were heading north, and I wanted so much to be one of them.

My husband appeared calm at sea. I noticed some of his confidence returning and an excitement within him at the prospect of heading north to the tropics, a place we both knew well. After a couple of weeks in the beautiful calm of the Clarence River, I was reminded it was time to think about heading north. Dozens of yachts were passing through, all heading north and over the bar. I paced the break wall and studied that bar more than I have critiqued anything in my life!

Opportunity after opportunity arrived to cross the bar in calm conditions. My husband would haul the anchor up and look so relieved. Then FEAR told me 'No'! Tears engulfed me and if I could describe how I felt in a word it would be 'frozen'. Sadly, I felt much more; failure, disappointment and immense sadness. I would glance at my husband as he re-anchored our boat in Iluka Bay, he was so patient with me, yet the disappointment showed in his eyes.

Many asked, 'Why are you still there?'

A severe infection with an impacted wisdom tooth led me to have surgery and I was so grateful for any reason not to leave the safety of the mighty Clarence! Winter months passed by and we navigated the river, not the tropics. I was dying inside. The blog I started with so much hope I abandoned, it spoke of our desire to live for our daughter and sail north.

I read of beautiful islands and tropical reefs others were exploring. I became convinced I was scared of the sea and our move to find some peace and meaning was a huge mistake. Yachts began returning south on their homeward journey… fear told me I was defeated and done.

Social situations were excruciating, unlike before. I was terrified I would transform into an emotional sobbing freak. What if anyone asked me: 'How many children do you have? Grandchildren?' Any light-hearted conversation on meeting fellow sailors would descend into a solemn response and I would expose my deepest sadness to a total stranger.

I became more isolated.

While in the Clarence we met two couples, on different boats, who had an incredible impact on us. Strangely both had lost close family traumatically and both befriended my husband and I in a very gentle way. They would be friends for a very long time. I began to consider that just perhaps there was another way and if I could only give myself time and stop trying to compare myself to prescribed notions of how we do this 'sailing thing', it may be possible? There began a journey of breaking through my fear. A slow and painful journey that continues today.

Summer arrived, and I had a plan! I would not cross the bar to leave the river, but my husband would, and I would meet him in Southport. From there we would explore Moreton Bay and surroundings and slowly move forward… not the way many others do, but in our own way. It took some convincing before my husband finally agreed. You see we were competent sailors and had spent years at sea in past decades. He was confused as to why I was so fearful. The plan was eventually implemented, and we found ourselves enjoying sailing Moreton Bay and its islands. Confidence grew within me and I started to ponder if it was the sea that I was so fearful of after all?

It is with some trepidation that I describe an event that highlighted that my fear was not derived from the sea but rather a fear of life itself and what it may unleash next. I sat in the cockpit one afternoon as my husband and Ivy went ashore. A couple of hours passed, and thoughts started to flood my brain; *'Where were they? What could have happened? Have they drowned? Has Ivy been bitten by a snake? Has my husband had a heart attack?'*

Thoughts hammered me relentlessly, as the sound of our outboard cut in on the horror in my mind. My husband and Ivy jumped onboard,

I was shaking and teary. I began to comprehend my fear and it made perfect sense now. Yes, the sea can be terrifying, as can roads, cars, and disease. If I was to crack through this fear, I needed to understand it. I needed to stop punishing myself and let go of other people's expectations. Knowing full well fear would grip me again, I was determined it would not keep me in its clutches. I owed it to myself, my husband, and our daughter to find a way. I was not weak or defeated. I think perhaps I was even a little brave for attempting to conquer this.

Forward three years and we are sailing north once again. We have not reached Cairns, but we will! It has been the slowest trip north anyone can envisage. I laugh now and I'm not ashamed. We have witnessed some of nature's uniquely beautiful wildlife and locations, this has warmed our souls. The sea and *Easter Rose* have given us time to reflect and breathe. I've met several friends on this sailing journey that I treasure.

Fear still haunts me. I know when we leave an anchorage Fear tells me, 'We may not get to our destination tonight'. I reply, 'I think we will'. When we arrive I feel very accomplished. I am no longer locked frozen by fear. Life will always terrify me as I have felt its fury at its harshest. I also know it's not weak to feel and face fear in your own, very individual, way. Facing fear at all and in whatever form, is indeed brave.

Bio: My name is Lanise Edwards. I am 53 years old. I live full-time aboard *SV Easter Rose* a 37-year-old monohull with my husband Tyler and our ageing dog Ivy. Currently we are travelling north and have been doing so very slowly for three years, with a few pauses in our journey. My experience of 'navigating fear' came from traumatic and tragic loss. This led me to have a need to identify what I feared and why. My journey has been very individual and I'm sure many others have found this too. I now enjoy our life on the sea with all its challenges and beauty.

13

The Anxious Mariner

by Lisa Mighetto

I am not what you would call a natural boater. I grew up in a desert town where my fellow Girl Scouts were trailblazers not mariners.

My friends engaged in many sports but none of them were sailors. Maybe that explains my lifelong fascination with water and attraction to boats of all kinds. The appeal has remained strong enough to carry me through various misadventures: ripping through the Golden Gate (small sailboat, high winds) trying to avoid the infamous Potato Patch; rowing a large fiberglass kayak in Puget Sound hoping to reach the shore before an expanding leak swamped the boat; navigating through a complex of reefs – and grounded sailboats – in search of a safe anchorage on Anegada Island in the BVIs; attempting to dock in the Swinomish Channel in currents so fierce that it took a crew of four plus a crowd of people on shore to pull the sailboat into the slip; a near knock-down on the west side of Vancouver Island; and crossing the Fraser River bar in seas so steep that I asked myself as I crawled along the floor of the cabin, *What am I doing here? Am I insane?* All of these situations had this in common: I was afraid, if not terrified. And I was not at the helm.

For years, I thought my fear stemmed from loss of control, of placing my fate in the hands of someone else. So, I armed myself with training, information, and careful, painstaking planning. I attended countless sailing seminars. While the physics of sailing interested me, I found it difficult to move beyond theoretical to practical applications. It seemed as though most people in the class had an affinity for the topic that I lacked. It took me a long time to grasp how concepts like 'velocity made good' translated into more effective and safer sailing. My favorite term was 'center of lateral resistance,' which always made me think of a place for free-thinking anarchists rather than how hydrodynamic forces affect the hull of a boat.

I participated in sailing seminars designed for women. One leader, seeking to soothe the fears of those lacking experience and confidence, had this advice for anxious mariners: 'When things get rough out there, say to yourself, "it's only wind; it's only water."' To me, that was like saying, 'It's only a serial killer'. Wind and water are very powerful and capricious forces – and I knew what they could do. In any case, learning to take the helm, use the radio, reef the sails, read weather patterns, rescue overboards, and approach a dock as well as a mooring buoy, helped with the outward signs of fear. I became more useful and competent, but I could not shake the anxiety completely.

Sailing literature helped by offering recognizable experiences. Looking beyond technical manuals and online how-to posts, I pored over accounts by Tania Abei, M. Wylie Blanchet, Kay Cottee, and Jessica Watson, as well as famous couples like the Smeetons, Hiscocks, and Pardeys. These writers present sailing as a grand adventure, for the most part meeting challenges with courage, grace, and strength of character. *But what if you are not a thrill seeker or just plain brave?*

Many writers suggest that the sea is best approached cautiously. Consider this chilling turn of phrase from Surfline, which recently viewed a series of unpredictable waves as 'nature in all its beautiful evil'. Or this passage from a loftier source – Coleridge's classic, The Rime of the Ancient Mariner, which reads like a horror story about a tormented sailor:

> Like one, that on a lonesome road
> Doth walk in fear and dread,
> And having once turned round walks on,
> And turns no more his head;
> Because he knows, a frightful fiend
> Doth close behind him tread.

I often picture myself as 'The Anxious Mariner' in a modern version of Coleridge's poem. As summed up simply in The Motion of the Ocean, my favorite cruising book, 'the sea is one fickle bitch.'

I started collecting stories from sailors I met on my cruises. While most described favorite anchorages and fun discoveries, some were downright scary. Even now the account of an evening sail on Lake Huron haunts me. It began as a tale of seasickness in a storm of unexpected intensity – and ended with a dead captain and an unprepared crew engaged in desperate navigation and docking. The point of the sailor's story: apparently terror can cure seasickness very quickly. What I took from it: a captain can be swept overboard, even with jacklines.

A similar conversation with an elderly mariner (old salt) at a yacht club bar began as a polite discussion of the Strait of Juan de Fuca and ended with a heartbreaking account of how his son lost his life on a solo crossing. Over time I detected patterns in disaster-at-sea tales. It seemed that often injury and loss of life occurs when sailors leave the vessel – voluntarily or involuntary. Life jackets are essential. And I have learned something else: the process of sharing experiences with other sailors produces empathy, camaraderie, and understanding.

My husband and I once met another couple while sailing in British Columbia. We bonded over dinner, rafting our boats. As the evening wore on we exchanged stories, and the topic turned to difficult passages. I confessed how nervous I was about navigating the currents and tides of BC and described a terrible crossing of the Strait of Georgia. For all my fear what really made me lose it was that I could not get the fiddles on the stove to work and could not make tea, as my boat careened wildly from side-to-side. The wife then began reminiscing about her mother, who had crossed the Atlantic in a small sailboat many years earlier. We were drinking wine and she became weepy. 'My mum sailed all the way across the ocean,' she marveled. 'And she did it without fiddles.' For some reason, we both found this hilarious and burst out laughing. We are friends to this day.

At a sailing club function a few nights ago I thought of this writing competition as I listened to a woman talk about what it was like to sail through the Tacoma Narrows during a recent squall. Looking around the table she ended by asking, 'Why do we do this?' The group erupted in laughter. The truth is that if you spend enough time on a boat eventually you will encounter a difficult situation – and you may well be afraid.

Why do I do this? Because it connects me with other people, with a community of sailors who, like me, are drawn to the water and to boats.

I have not conquered my fear, but I accept it. And my anxiety produces a heightened sense of awareness – when I am on a boat I am hyper conscious of all that is around me. I imagine this is something akin to what hunters and anglers experience. I encounter nature in all its sublime variety and my preparations indicate the level of my respect and awe, if not reverence. And I would not trade my sailing life for anything.

Bio: Lisa Mighetto is a historian based in Seattle, USA, where she has sailed the Salish Sea for several decades. Her writing has appeared in Sierra, Pacific Yachting, 48 Degrees North, and other publications. For more information see:

http://dire2260.wixsite.com/lisamighetto

14

Up the Creek Without a Paddle

by Laurel Cooper

Facing your fears. Thinking about it, I realised that many negative Fs were involved, like Frailty, Failure, and Fatigue.

Nelson Mandela once said, 'Courage is not the absence of fear but the triumph over it.'

I learnt to sail on the Norfolk Broads as a child. Sailing on inland waters was the first of my triumphs against fear, it brought Familiarity with the water, often fear of the unknown is the worst. So is fear of Failure, which makes learning and experience so important. When it came to ocean voyaging in middle age I was again facing the unknown. In my case there was a fear of Frailty, as I am small of stature and born with a dislocated hip. I mustered the antidotes — positive F's — Faith: in my husband, whom I had known and admired for his seamanship for 25 years, in the boat he had designed, and we had largely built, Food, Friends and Family, Familiarity (this must be earned), and Fortitude.

A long hot summer saw six of us, including our son, setting out on my first ocean voyage, leaving Lowestoft on the 20th of June, non-stop to Gibraltar (we hoped), on our strongly built 58-foot steel ketch. That hope was scuppered when a fractured fuel line had us into Boulogne (in thick fog) for repairs. Then, off the Channel Islands, the propeller shaft failed, and we put into St Peter Port, Guernsey. As we had a cat on board (one-eyed Nelson) we were not allowed alongside but had to anchor off. An engineer replaced the sheared bolt. Surely it would last until we could haul out. We set off again for Gibraltar.

The Bay of Biscay strikes fear into many a brave heart. On the 6th and 7th of July it lived up to its reputation with a two-day gale, that set us into the Bay with strong winds from the south west. It was choppy, not to say rough, but despite the high seas the ship behaved well; we went into two-man watches, and between us managed to produce copious and enjoyable meals, which went a long way to boosting morale, as did the fact that we were coping well, thanks partly to food.

We flew down the coast of Portugal with strong winds and heavy seas. Rounded Cape St Vincent on the 10th of July and entered Gibraltar on the 12th July.

For the next five weeks we enjoyed the coast of Spain, Ibiza, and Majorca and arrived in Mahon (Menorca) on August 17th.

We sailed up Mahon harbour close hauled on the port tack. Preparing to motor into a berth, the shaft coupling went, as it had done off the Channel Islands. This time it slipped back and fouled the rudder, and we were forced to anchor without the engine. Our son dived and tried to shift the shaft, so did Dennis, the unofficial port officer for any boat with a British flag, who had greeted us on arrival. No luck.

Clearly our boat was going nowhere. After a voyage of 2,508 nautical miles from Lowestoft, including a non-stop stretch from Guernsey to Gibraltar of 1,280 nautical miles, which made us all accredited Ocean Sailors, it was summer's end. The crew, including our son, went their ways.

We fell in love with the island and consolidated our friendship with Dennis and Dereka at their restaurant, 'Scandals'. Dennis was a sailor and knew these waters well, and he and Bill clicked immediately, as did I with Dereka, both of us hooked on food and the cooking thereof.

September brought the first storms. During a violent gale, neighbouring vessel *Venilia* dragged its anchor while they were dining ashore and we rescued it successfully. They repaid us when our batteries suddenly discharged a few days later, and a lead snaked over our decks from their boat to ours to recharge them.

Dennis made several attempts to remove the shaft, finally succeeding with a car jack. Seamanship is endless resourcefulness. We took the shaft to the Naval Dockyard. Given notice to leave our berth, a bit of beseeching won us until October 7th. We then shifted alongside an amenable fishing boat, helped by Toful of the pilot boat, with whom we had made friends.

October was a herald of winter. There were more storms.

We had a fire in the engine room, successfully extinguished by Bill who had a lot of experience fighting fires at sea in the Navy.

'My stupidity,' he said.

The paraffin container had leaked onto the batteries below, and the ensuing arcing had caused the fire.

'What was I thinking of, storing paraffin above the battery bank?'

We transferred the paraffin into a sturdier container and moved it to a safer place. As usual there was a lot of cleaning up to do.

The following day we visited the dockyard, where our shaft was ready, and made arrangements to get it to the boat. There would be no charge, said the dockyard officer. Embarrassing, and suspicious.

Dennis helped us to reinstall the shaft, and it became clear that the Spanish Navy had failed to repair it. Diplomacy, which Bill was familiar with from his days in the Navy, meant that face must be saved and nothing said. No wonder there was no charge.

We held a Council of War at 'Scandals', over Dereka's delicious chicken curry.

'Barcelona, then, under sail; 172 nautical miles,' said Dennis. 'We've completed more than 2,000 miles so far: What hairy moments have we had along the way?'

The fuel line, fog at Boulogne, one of the crew hit his head on a steel rail and needed butterfly stitches, sailing into St Peter Port with a broken shaft, storm in the Bay of Biscay.

'All we need is a weather window.'

I was not so sure.

Bill said, 'Dennis thinks we can do this. I know I can. Do you trust me?'

'Forever,' I said. 'And the boat too. It's me I doubt. All summer six people on board. Now just you and me, up the creek without a paddle, and winter's coming on. You'll be fine, but am I strong enough?'

'You got me through depression,' he said. 'Takes a lot of strength to do that. And a sense of humour!' He laughed. 'Who needs a paddle when we've got sails?'

I no longer worried about my physical Frailty. I had found over the summer that I was stronger than I thought, and on a boat arms were what mattered, not legs, and I had strong arms. In years to come I would be amazed and delighted at the people I met, with handicaps that made mine look like a gnat bite; cheerfully sailing and making successful voyages.

We had to wait out more gales, but the first week in November Dennis reported, 'South westerlies for the next few days. They'll blow you to Barcelona.'

Early on the 10th of November we singled up, made plain sail with a reef in the main, weighed anchor and set off down six kilometres of channel to the sea. Once there, we rounded the island and set our course to 340 degrees, with a strong south-westerly breeze, close hauled and going well.

At sunset we made the unwelcome discovery that the engines would not start, we needed them to charge the batteries. The navigation lights lasted the night, and when below we used the oil lamp.

The following day began with no wind, but soon a light breeze began, which became a stormy south-westerly, with rain and rafales (gusts). We had cold food, to save the batteries for the nav lights, which did not last the second night, despite us switching them off when there was no shipping on the radar.

The third day began with no wind and an uncomfortably rough sea. Our progress was slow, but we were not far off now. When the wind came in it veered towards the north and we had to tack, right up to the harbour mouth, and into Barcelona's busy harbour among huge warships and commercial shipping. We arrived with great relief at the Darsena Nazionale at 1600 hours, where we plugged into shore power.

At last we could relax and have a tot. Bed beckoned after three days of watches and naps taken in the deckhouse to be on call for whoever was at the wheel. (We were one of the first to have a proper sized bed in our aft cabin, with a padded divider slotted down the middle at sea.) The cat was already at home there.

'Do you want another tot?' asked Bill. 'To celebrate?'

'No,' I said, 'Let's go to bed.' With his arms wrapped around me, I felt no fear of the future.

So, my lovelies: Collect your F's like a bunch of Flowers –

Faith, Food, Friends, Family, Familiarity, and Fortitude, and use them to fight the Foe, and if you feel the flutter in your stomach descending to your boots when you get the hurricane warning: it's all FEASIBLE, and can even be FUN.

Bio: I was born in Gorleston, Norfolk UK in 1929 with a dislocated hip, spent two-and-a-half years in orthopaedic hospital followed by leg irons for several years. My wartime education was disjointed.

Despite everything I learnt to sail on my father's boat on the Norfolk Broads, where I met Bill, racing his dinghy in the same waters, Bill skippering my father's boat to win many races. We were sixteen and became pretty much inseparable. In 1947 Bill went to Dartmouth Naval College and I went to Leeds College of Art. Thenceforth we met when we could, continuing to sail both on the Broads and the South Coast.

I graduated in 1951, by which time Bill was a Lieutenant and had been a Navigator with the Far Eastern Fleet for a couple of years.

On his return in 1952, we married and had two children, and followed the fleet for a while. After 15 years Bill left the Navy with the rank of Lieut-Commander. He went into the city as he had a talent for investments, but after some years came close to breakdown as he hated his job. He quit in 1972 and we began to build our own boat, which occupied us for the next four years.

We sailed away in 1976 on what was to be a cruise of nearly 100,000 miles under sail which lasted until we were into our eighties, first on *Fare Well*, a 58-foot ketch which Bill designed, then the Dutch barge *Hosanna* for the next twenty years, and then on *Faraway*, our geriatric boat, also designed by Bill, which we used on the European canals.

After ten years of experience we wrote 'Sell Up and Sail' (the Times newspaper called it the Sailing Bible), which became a best seller and is still popular more than thirty years on.

We wrote several more books.

I am now eighty-nine years old and live ashore. We will write no more books, as Bill died two years ago, and we wrote as a team; though the illustrations were mine.

However, I still write articles for the Nautical Press.

For further details see:
http://billandlaurelcooper.com/

15

I'm Afraid of Waves

by Denise Lowden

Hi, my name is Denise and I'm afraid of waves.

Silence.

Whales, she said whales!

Um no, I said waves, and besides who could be scared of whales, they are delightful. Yes, waves.

More silence.

You do realise you live on a boat, you are a SCUBA instructor, and you've spent your life on or near the water? You've windsurfed, stand-up-paddle boarded, white-water rafted, canoed, and snorkelled your way around the world. Bloody hell, your nickname as a dive instructor was Ocean Girl! You can't be serious?

Yup, deadly serious. But, just because I am scared of waves doesn't mean I don't love the water. Let me explain a little further.

Waves are unpredictably inconsistent, and I don't like that about them. It took a particular water-based event for me to 'remember' that I don't like waves. As dive instructors, my husband and I were looking for an activity to do when it was too rough to go diving. Surfing seemed like the obvious choice, so down we went to Middleton Beach, Western Australia, where we rented some boards and paddled out. About 30 minutes into it though I 'remembered' that I don't like waves.

Now, to be clear, teaching diving in South Australia is no walk in the park, the gulf is a particularly dodgy bit of water and it is often, well, not great. But as a diver or instructor you spend very little time on the surface, and being under the waves is wonderful, it doesn't bother me at all. Having a regulator and BCD (Buoyancy Control Device) means that even if a wave crashes over me I have control of both my breathing and my ability to stay afloat.

Being in waves and surf though, is very uncomfortable. Waves are very powerful, and they take away any sense of control that you might have.

We own a catamaran precisely because I do not like boats that heel, I don't like being that close to the waves. Our catamaran elevates me a little higher and the lack of tilt makes me seem more in control (even though I am well aware it is an artificial sense of security).

Our first test passage, an overnight sail to East Diamond Islet from Airlie Beach (some 220 nautical miles) was a real test of my ability to talk myself into doing something that made me feel uncomfortable. And I found that rather than the length of time in rough weather making me feel more unsettled, the fact that I couldn't stop, couldn't escape, actually helped. The relentless waves bashing the side of our catamaran gave me confidence, with each hit, we didn't die, the boat didn't sink, and I started to realise that both the boat and I were stronger than I thought.

A recent passage to Norfolk Island from Elizabeth Reef pushed my mental strength a LOT further. The wind and waves built up rapidly as night approached. My husband kept looking at me and asking what was wrong, oddly for me (a chatterbox at the best of times) I was near mute. I was certain that should I actually express how scared and unsettled I felt I would cry.

I was positive crying was not going to help. As luck would have it my husband was due to go to bed and I would be up on watch alone in the pitch dark (of course no moon) in the worst weather I'd ever experienced onboard.

The first hour was the toughest, the second (having not died or sunk) slightly better, by the third I was almost back to normal. I was soaking wet and my hands and feet were cramped from bracing and holding on, but I had done it – alone. Listening to music and singing helped immensely. I had dabbled with Audible books on other overnight passages, and Jessica Watson's book, True Spirit, about her solo unassisted sail around the world was great to listen to on our lovely passage to Lord Howe Island. Can I say though, Ellen MacArthur's book, Full Circle, was a nightmare. In no particular order, she dismasted, pitchpoled and rolled a variety of boats way too many times for my liking. I had to turn her book off multiple times and change to music as each catastrophe occurred. I eventually finished that book during the daylight in good weather. Word of advice – it is a good book, do NOT listen to it at night in bad weather unless you are seriously insane.

My husband later told me he found it incredibly difficult to leave me up there looking as I did.

Looking at our YouTube footage weeks later (no we didn't shoot any of me actually mute) I was shocked to see that even on the following day I looked shattered and exhausted. It's rare that you get to step outside yourself and see what you look like when you are struggling. It was not a pretty picture and that was 18 hours later!

My advice for overcoming your fears is to try to understand what it is exactly that you are scared of. *Am I really afraid of waves?* At the end of the day it's just water. It boils down to the fact that I am afraid of the loss of control and the feeling of insignificance that waves bring.

If you can, start small (short trips, small waves), listen to music, sing and dance (the singing and dancing bit is best done in private if your voice and dancing skills are anything like mine), and don't be too hard on yourself. I am sure there are more mute days in my future and as we continue to explore the world, there will be bigger waves and worse weather.

Will I be able to talk myself around? I think so. If nothing else, I am willing to try.

Bio: Denise Lowden is a registered nurse who has spent the last 12 years as a plastic surgery practice manager and CEO. A PADI Staff Instructor (lapsed) and wanna-be chef. Denise (and husband Jamie) cast off in January set to explore the world both above and below the water.
Follow their adventures: lukimyu.com.au

16

Getting Better All The Time

by Joy B. Carey

I was a white-knuckled-starter to sailing. Heeling over took my stomach with it and the sudden flapping of sails scared me senseless. My first date with my husband was on a fast and sleek classic sloop, *Scheherezade*, and he put her through the paces while I hung on for dear life. Still, I was convinced that life on a boat was a romantic notion. We'd be anchored in serene coves, in exotic countries with birds chirping on shore and dolphins playing nearby. Sure. That would, of course, be years later, after saving enough money to buy a bare hull, completing and outfitting the boat in a yard, birthing a first child, saving more money, and finally splashing the boat. This was the late 1970s and the cool thing to do was build everything yourself. Which we did.

We then sailed up the Pacific Coast of the United States. It seemed it was more prudent with a baby on board and my lack of sailing skills to not get too far away from land. One of the first nights at sea, I was gripped with fear; not because anything was going wrong but because it was new, strange, the sky was dark, the sea was deep, the waves were... actually not that bad at all. But I was remorseful that I was subjecting my infant to the possibility of dangerous conditions. Said infant, however, could be found at any given time teething on her dad's Topsiders or sleeping peacefully spread-eagled in the v-berth.

Sure, there were some idyllic anchorages. Back then, you could anchor in Catalina Harbor, hike into The Isthmus while wild goats bleated on the hillsides and shaggy buffalo chomped on the grasses within an arm's length. You could have a chat with the locals while sipping a soda on a rock wall. As we headed further north, however, things began to change. We had to round capes like Cape Mendocino, with notorious reputations. We rounded that cape on a foggy night with flat seas, bell buoys clanging, foghorns moaning in the distance, and a silhouetted pair of whales pulling out in front of our bow, headed toward the moon. Real scary stuff.

The weather could turn, however, rather quickly. Days of sloppy seas, uncomfortable in our 32-foot sloop, *Fenwick Light*, were punctuated with crossing river bars.

One of those crossings occurred at the Siuslaw River on a dark and stormy night, falling in behind a ship when we couldn't find the channel markers. As we did, we strayed into shallower waters, which kept getting shallower while my voice kept getting higher as I called out the single digit depths to Jim at the helm. About then, we heard a voice on the VHF call the Coast Guard and tell them he thought there was a sailboat in a little trouble behind him. We broke in to let the Coast Guard know we weren't in trouble, just tired, and we couldn't find the channel markers. The 'coasties' told us that the channel markers had been temporarily removed so the dredge could do its work. We were behind a dredge, not a ship. Well that made sense.

We continued in, anchored, and as I sat exhausted, trying to fix a nominal dinner and feed our daughter, I said, perhaps it was time to sell the boat. No, I actually said something more like, 'I hate this! I want off this boat. Let's sell it now, to anyone with an offer.' Jim, of course, was not deterred and referenced Eric Hiscock, who, in one of his books, had stated that sailing up the Pacific coast of the US was one of the toughest voyages he and Susan had made and had it been his first passage, as it was indeed mine, he might have given up cruising altogether.

Knowing that Susan Hiscock had made it through this – even by their estimation – tough passage, energized my spinal fluid a bit and we finally made it to Bellingham, Washington.

We kind of made our home there, Jim got a job and we birthed another child, made two more trips up and down the coast to Baja, Mexico and finally wised up and got a bigger boat.

Every time we set to sea, I had matured a bit in handling the conditions we came up against. As waves increased in size with a crossing, I found that my fear level was moderated when I realized nothing bad was happening. Each time, I would think if it didn't get any worse than this, then I was okay. Repeat.

The first serious test came when we entered the region off Nicaragua known as the Papagayos. On the chart, the Gulf of Papagayo was 17 miles across. Not such a big deal; we could handle that. In actuality, the Papagayos range from the coast of Nicaragua to Costa Rica with trade winds accelerating down the west side of the mountains and fanning out over the coastal waters out to 100 miles or more. They hit a contrary current and make steep standing waves.

First, we ran with the waves, but the next morning we realized we would miss Costa Rica altogether if we kept on that course, so we fired up the engine and beat our way to the coast. We pounded into the 15-foot waves, green water barreling over the bow and down the sides into our cockpit, floating the teak grating up around the pedestal. I didn't like it much. I liked it even less when night fell, and I couldn't exactly see the waves coming. I'd get over one, two, then get slammed on the bow by the third wave in line. I began to think of my two girls and what I was putting them through.

Jim came up to take the helm and I promised to keep talking to him and handing him mugs of tea, so he could stay awake. Later, I realized this was not practical as I would have to take the wheel at first light and I would be exhausted. So, being the great mom that I was, I bundled up our 13-year-old daughter in foulies and sent her out to sit in the corner under the dodger to keep talking and handing Dad his mugs of tea while I got a short rest. She was instructed to wake up her sister in about an hour-and-a half to take her place and then it would be light enough for me to take over. When I got up I looked out to see that my 11-year-old was sitting in the cockpit in oversized foulies, bare feet sticking out, one hand on the wheel steering over the waves with rolls of green water bursting into the cockpit. Jim was asleep in the corner. I was horrified. *What had I done to my girls?* Kelly saw me and broke into a big smile, 'Hi Mom,' she said cheerfully and then ducked when another wave toppled over her. They had handled the first big test at sea better than I did. We made it through two more days of this and then safely in to Playa Blanca.

Since then we have sailed over 60,000 miles around the world. I have handled the helm in the outskirts of a cyclone in the Java Sea. I was at the helm while we battled a ferocious squall at Helen Reef that nearly drove us on the reef. Recently, I took over the helm after we were violently capsized by a rogue wave just 150 miles from completing our circumnavigation and steered for the better part of six hours in steep seas, the largest I had ever seen in nearly 40 years of cruising. When that was over I realized that I had not panicked, not for a second, as I concentrated on keeping our stern to the waves. We lost our boat that day. That broke my heart.

I don't hate the ocean. Well, I hate that one wave. And, truthfully, now I would be scared to go out to that part of the blue planet again. The waters out of Washington and Oregon are known to be treacherous at times. But when I see posts from cruising friends in wonderful places, I immediately begin to think how great it would be to go out there. There's so much more to see. Maybe, just maybe, I'm not quite done yet.

Bio: Jim and I built our first boat, *Fenwick Light*, from a bare hull in the 70s and sailed up and down the West Coast of the US, into Canada and as far south as La Paz, Baja, Mexico. The pull to set out for distant places was too strong to be resisted and we bought a bigger boat, *Kelaerin*, in 1991 and sailed down the western coasts again, through the Panama Canal to Florida. Although not specifically intending to do a circumnavigation, that is what we eventually did, sailing nearly 70,000 miles and visiting more than 50 countries along the way. We lost our boat just 150 miles short of completing the non-circumnavigation when we were violently capsized by another rogue wave.

http://cruisinginkelaerin.blogspot.com/

17

Overboard on Barge Life

by Hilary Hunter

'Have you always wanted to live on a boat?' must be the question I've been asked more times than I can count, since I began my life afloat. After all, it's a natural assumption when you radically change your lifestyle midlife, for many to think it unusual. Such a life-changing move would be too scary for many, so naturally it was assumed to be a familiar place for me.

I have always lived by the coast, enjoyed walks on the beach, and admired beautiful vessels. My experience of being afloat had been limited to the Larne-Stranraer ferry, and I was known for not having sea legs! So, ending my downsizing mission in a 120-year-old Dutch sailing barge certainly filled me with many fears.

Fear of the unknown is probably the greatest hindrance to many, if not most, people's hopes and dreams. I was buying something I knew nothing about, to live a lifestyle I had never even contemplated before. My family told me I was throwing my money away, taking huge risks on a dream of a more planet-friendly home. They foretold disaster at every opportunity. I stalled this fear by drawing a comparison to a classic car – something worth restoring, treasuring and most of all enjoying the use of.

Of course, the fact that she was old, added another item to my fear list. Purchasing something you know nothing about, which has been used and abused for many an eon, can be fraught with pitfalls. In this case, research was my answer. I soon found out that newly built barges could expect to survive around 25 years, whilst an old lady like mine could be likened to those wonderful old Volvo cars that start first time after being in a barn for decades. She was built by experts when life on the water was commonplace. I felt a sense of sanctuary once aboard. This old lady was going to outlive me, for sure.

Fear of falling overboard or losing something precious in an accidental offering to the 'Water Gods', is probably the most obvious one for any landlubber. Fortunately, my barge had a reassuring safety railing, wide gangways, and a sturdy reliability that comes with a riveted iron hull. A long boat hook stowed close to hand ensured anything that fell in could be easily retrieved. So far, this essential implement has rescued a hatch cover blown off in a storm, the dog who misjudged the jump ashore, the cat who thought mud in a drying berth could be walked across, and the same (somewhat senile) cat who misjudged his ability to jump aboard the neighbour's, much higher, boat.

This big old iron lady had survived two world wars, what could scare me in such a blessed survivor?

My chosen electrician brought my next fear aboard. Opening the first electrical junction box, he gasped in horror at the tangle of spaghetti-like wires confronting him. This reaction continued as he worked his way all through the boat. He even took to calling me at odd hours, just to check I was ok, whilst he transformed this nightmare to British Standards. His associate soon ensured my gas system would not blow me to kingdom-come either. Danger seemed to be forever trying to sink my optimism.

Another contender in the 'silly question most asked' competition was the one about cold and damp. As my little furry companions, dog and cat, toasted themselves by the multi-fuel stove on our first night afloat, I was glad to discount this fear very swiftly. Anyone living in a small space will know how cosy it gets, and as the warmth spread around the cabins, I knew damp conditions had a fight on their hands.

That first dark and stormy winter's night was enough to strike fear in many hearts, even those safely ashore in bricks and mortar. Tucked up snugly in a very un-boat-like double berth, the noise of water slapping the heavy timber rudder, rattling the tonne weight of the leeboards, and flapping rigging wires against the mast, I should have been ruing the day someone suggested I buy a barge. Yet strangely, this wonderful elderly Dutch lady reassured me with her sturdiness and slow rhythmic rocking. Other lighter vessels nearby bounced and bucked, straining their ropes fighting to be free. Winds howled, and waves crashed but this wonderful old girl had seen it all before. Her calm presence reassured me, and I slept peacefully, secure in the knowledge of safety in her hull.

Several years have now passed since that first night. Any fears I may have had, have been put to rest with the joy of misty sunrises over the river, stunning views from my rooftop beanbag seat and the closeness to wildlife that's not usually so close. Gone are the fears for safety, the anxiety of money spent generously, and ignorance of nautical terms and sailing skills. Only one fear now exists in my mind. That of the future, when I am too frail to maintain her and ill health drives me ashore. Someday, I must face my biggest fear yet. I must pass custodianship of my old Dutch lady to her next owners. But until then, together we are fearless.

Bio: Irish woman Hilary Hunter, midlife tree hugger and novice sailor, started her sailing barge love affair just four years ago. Now devoted to her own ship *Drie Gebroeders*, she writes from below deck on planet-friendly matters.

https://hilaryhunterwriter.com/

18

The Lesson

by Clare Earley

'Feel the Fear and Do It Anyway'
Susan Jeffers

Timing is everything, and everything had come together just in time. We had settled on our cute little timber yacht on Christmas Eve, driven to the Gold Coast for a family Christmas Day, and now on Boxing Day we were heading out to meet friends at Stradbroke Island. There were four of us aboard and the day was picture postcard perfect, except for the fact that there was only the tiniest zephyr of a breeze. We escaped the confinement of the leads, hoisted our tatty little sails, turned off the noisy engine and were sailing, albeit at about 2 knots, but who cares how fast you are going when in heaven!

Every time a slight gust passed across our decks another fleck of paint would fly away – we really had some work to do to restore her to her former glory – but for now we were enjoying our first experience of the peace and tranquillity that is sailing.

I will be honest with you and admit that I did not trust that my husband was going to be up for the Skipper role as I was not sure how good at this sailing thing he really was. So, we had my father, who had sailed thousands of nautical miles, and his wife, who had never even been on a boat, to accompany us on this, our maiden voyage. Later, I would learn how wrong I was about my husband's ability, and I now trust him with my life.

Insanely black clouds loomed ahead and the threat of what was in store bore down upon us as thick as the air that now surrounded us. Sails were dropped after encouraging the engine back into life, everything was stowed below, and we kept pushing on. We watched helplessly as a yacht coming towards us had their dinghy flung into their cockpit as they were almost knocked down… but not quite, instead they were then pushed onto a sandbank.

We collided with the force of Mother Nature. Our engine was not powerful enough to propel us forward against the wind, so we turned and motored with it. The wind came and went, and we were unscathed. We turned the boat around and continued on. Next came the rain – it felt like hail on our skin and hurt so bad, but it was hurting our poor girl also as we found ourselves powerless to push through it. Once again, we turned and went with the weather until it was over.

Throughout all of this I found that I wasn't terrified, a little scared perhaps, but in comforting our guest, I stayed strong, positive and quite okay. The boys had taken care of everything on decks and while we were tired and sore by the time we finally made it to Deanbilla Bay, we were all okay.

Next stop: The Wide Bay Bar! Our first major trip away was three weeks in the Great Sandy Straits and we were both more than a bit nervous about our first crossing of the infamous bar. It was, however, almost perfect, largely due to the fact that we had thoroughly researched the best conditions to cross. So, we enjoyed a smooth and uneventful passage both in and out. During this time, we fell in love with the life we had worked so hard for. My heart was heavy, and tears streamed down my face uncontrollably for a large part of the return trip. I was still a terrible sailor and complained to the Skipper all the time. The boat and I felt like friends and when she was under pressure so was I, the only difference was that she would take it all in her stride and I would open my mouth.

The second time heading to the Great Sandy Straits from Mooloolaba was very different as we didn't know if or when we would return. We had decluttered our lives and everything we owned was either in a tiny garden shed under the house which we had rented out, or onboard with us. I don't think I was aware at the time that a cocktail of excitement, both joyous and nervous, along with the busyness of completing all that needed to be done, whilst staying with friends and saying our farewells, all masked the fact that something inside me was changing.

A false start to our voyage, with an unexpected wind change – 25 knots from the north – saw our journey postponed for a couple of days. But we eventually made it across the bar and into one of our favourite places – The Great Sandy Straits. I relished the clock-less, traffic-less, freedom, but began getting stressed about odd things and teary at the drop of a hat. This continued for the three months it took us to meander up the coast to the Whitsunday Islands and it was at times, debilitating. When the conditions were lively I developed panic attacks, which made me completely useless. On our way from Bundaberg to Pancake Creek the swell and wind gusts were so bad that our autopilot could not keep us on course and my Skipper had to tiller steer by hand for almost the entire passage. At one stage he asked me to take the tiller, so he could relieve himself. I was paralysed by fear and just couldn't do it, before I knew it we were yelling at each other and all I could do was find him a bucket. Another time, we had planned a romantic evening and as the sun set with us enjoying a sundowner or two in the cockpit I developed a terrible migraine with the pain searing up through the back of my head like somebody was slicing open my skull with a hot blade. I could not understand what was going on with my body, why was it rejecting me when we had fought to get here and were now supposed to be living the dream? For the previous few years, whilst not by any means being a great sailor, I had never had any of these problems.

Languishing in my own self-pity, I was devastated when anchored off Airlie Beach one afternoon the Skipper announced, 'We've done it now, let's go home, back to the house and our lives as they were'.

I hadn't noticed the toll that my issues were having on him, because we were actually having an amazing time in spite of my apparent issues. I was really good at this life and enjoying it, for the most part. We had met some wonderful people and had some truly enlightening experiences so why did he want to turn around and give it all up? I acted immediately – spoke to people about it and was coming up with a plan when it hit me like a bolt of lightning: That's what I did. What I was good at. My childhood was not overly positive so in adulthood I tend to help others and fix their problems. When somebody asks what makes me happy? The answer is always the same – as long as the people I love are happy and I can do things to aide in their happiness, then I am happy. Now, here I find myself living my own dream, doing something for me for once in my life and my body reacts: No, you don't! You don't deserve to be happy! Then, because I do it anyway, it comes up with both mental and physical punishments.

All this may sound a little flaky, but I know I am not the only one out here on the water who is affected by similar issues. We hear it all the time, women who think they are not good enough physically, or don't have the mental aptitude for this sailing life. I have come a long way and am still learning to deal with it. My wonderful Skipper and I still live aboard – on a much larger yacht now, but we talk all the time and now he doesn't show his frustration with my silly questions in quite the same way. I am the *'When are we putting the sails up? Down? How many? There's another boat coming (5 miles away)'* kind of person and even though I still find myself asking these questions sometimes, now I can also laugh at the ridiculousness of them. He is very patient with me and often reminds me to take my rescue remedy even before I think of it, he is kind and thoughtful and without him I wouldn't be here, but we make a great team and encourage and support each other.

Yes, we have been through other storms, even dragged our anchor across the bay in the middle of the night, stopping merely a few feet from another boat, but now that my fear of living is under control I am able to take these challenges on board as they arise and, on our boat, both Skipper and First Mate face each day together.

Bio: Clare Earley came to sailing later in life and together with her husband Graham, live aboard their 42 ft yacht *Mai Tintola.* Currently on anchor in the Brisbane river while her husband works in his trade, Clare is establishing her handcraft business Seabear Creations and enjoying sailing beautiful Moreton Bay. The couple are planning another cruise up the Queensland Coast next year and hopefully offshore in the future. They finally found *Phoe* a car which they are happy with – a little black Merc no less. But Clare is always so happy to come home to her little floating sanctuary!

19

Squash Zone in the Pacific

by Ann Lange

We left Bora Bora, one of the western-most islands in French Polynesia, and headed for one of the Cook Islands, Suwarrow. It was just my husband, Barry, and me in our Fast Passage 39, a cutter-rigged, double-ender with a small offshore cockpit, built in 1985 and designed for blue water sailing. We had owned her for three years but never had cause to test her in bad weather. We departed on a bright sunny day, with a weather forecast indicating good sailing conditions for our seven hundred nautical mile journey.

The ITCZ, or the Inter Tropical Convergence Zone, had moved south of the equator and collided with a high-pressure system. This phenomenon, referred to as a squash zone, had not been forecast and the weather deteriorated dramatically. At the peak of the disturbance, we had 30-40 knots of sustained wind with seas to 20 feet.

As the wind began to increase and the sea state became violent we reduced sail, putting a reef in the main, rolling in the jib and hoisting the staysail. We were hammered by squall after squall with gusty winds and driving rain. In the cloudy conditions, we couldn't see the squalls coming. We continued to reduce sail; putting the third reef in the main and hanking-on the storm staysail until finally, we pulled the main down altogether, secured it, and ran under storm staysail alone. The only way to reduce sail further would have been to continue under bare poles. The boat was surfing down the backs of waves at 11 knots, which was alarming because our theoretical hull speed is only 7.5 knots.

On watch in the middle of the night, I was very apprehensive about our situation. I was tethered to the boat to port and starboard to reduce the risk of being tossed around in the confused seas. I clung to the wheel. The electric auto pilot could not steer through the storm; the seas were too confused. The mechanical wind vane self-steering was also overpowered – hand steering was our only option.

I could hear the waves coming but I could not see them, the clouds obscured the moon and it was pitch black. The waves sounded so powerful, like a freight train bearing down on us. The sound would swell until the waves were propelled under the boat. The force of the water would lift our vessel in a surge up the wave and then she would careen down, in a heart stopping swoop. Every once in a while, a rogue wave would hit us on the beam. BAM! Gallons of salt water came crashing into the cockpit, scaring the bejesus out of me. When those waves hit, I was soaked from head to toe and the cockpit was half full of water.

If I lost control of the boat and it rolled would I get stuck underneath with my tether wrapped around a winch and be unable to get free? Would I drown? If tension on the shrouds or the stays became too great, would the mast come down? Would I be crushed by the falling spar, or would the shrouds ensnare and trap me before my husband could set me free? Could one of those rogue waves wash me overboard? If I was washed overboard, could I get my captain's attention, so he could assist me before I was dragged underwater by the runaway boat? What if I lost control of the helm and accidentally gybed? Would the preventer line snap? Would the boom swing across the cockpit with enough force to take my head off? All these anxieties surfaced during those long, dark, terrifying hours.

The last thing I wanted to do was get broadside to the waves, a roll over was much more likely if that happened. I continued to wrestle with the wheel, staring at the compass so that I could maintain the correct course. The thought that I only had to hold on for two hours instead of the usual four made the task slightly less onerous. Even so, the concentration required to maintain the course was intense.

I am an optimist by nature so dwelling on my fears was not my usual state of mind, but how do you train your subconscious to ignore the 'what ifs' and concentrate on getting the job done? I knew that I could not give into my fears and cower below. My husband, Barry, needed his rest so that we could both make rational decisions if the weather worsened. I considered the positives. We were going in the right direction and the boat seemed to be handling the weather. It came down to me. *Could I hold on to the wheel and not let my mind dwell on what might be?*

I was so tired from the lack of sleep and dealing with the conditions that all my focus, strength, and will-power were needed just to steer. My terrifying thoughts faded into the background, I could not deal with them now, I could not waste any effort indulging those uncertainties. Fear served no purpose here, giving in to my insecurities would only paralyze me and cripple my efforts.

Once my shift was over, I headed below, so relieved not to have the responsibility for steering the boat anymore. Shortening the shifts from four hours to two had been a good decision. Even if we did not sleep on the off-watch, at least we could dry off, change out of our sopping, salt encrusted clothes, lie down and rest. While I lay there trying to relax, I let go and put my life in my husband's hands, as he had put his in mine. I had all the confidence in the world in him and I realized in that moment that he must have that same confidence in me.

After three days, the storm gradually blew itself out and we survived without any mishaps. I had conquered my fears of being knocked down, dismasted or rolled, by parking my anxieties and focusing on what mattered. We practiced good safe sailing methods. We'd adjusted to the deteriorating weather by reefing early, by changing to the hanked-on sails before there was a risk of being washed away on the foredeck. We'd also adjusted our watch schedule, reducing the time we had to deal with the elements. We always had a good maintenance plan for the sails, standing rigging and turnbuckles right down to the smallest of cotter pins – all those items that would keep us sailing, safe, and alive.

Our boat behaved beautifully, doing what she was designed to do. I had gained a tremendous amount of confidence in my ability to endure in less than ideal conditions. I had learned to trust my mind and my body to deal with whatever the ocean could throw at me. Ever since our experience in the squash zone, I realized that I had conquered my fears of dealing with rough conditions and I would never abandon our boat unless I had to step-up off her.

Bio: Ann Lange, *SV Cat's-Paw IV*, Fast Passage 39.
Ann completed a twelve-year circumnavigation in May 2017. She intends to continue coastal sailing, with her husband Barry, along the Pacific Coast of Mexico during the cold Canadian winters for the next few years.

Ann submits articles to The Bluewater Cruising Association for publication in their magazine Currents.

http://annoeyk.blogspot.com

20

Night Watch

by Penny Talbot

'Face your fears'... for me boating has been all about facing my fears.

From the time I set foot on our first boat (we were what, twenty-five?) to three years ago when we accomplished something I had never imagined – cruising the Pacific coast to Mexico – there have been many fears that needed facing. And yet, here we were, setting the bar higher as we pushed ourselves a little harder and further.

'Overnight passage' was our last great hurdle, and one that we had acknowledged but never found time to address. We were scheduled to leave for Mexico in the fall of 2015 on the Cubar* cruise, and our N46 *Northern Ranger* was still in Canada. Timing was everything – we needed to avoid storms and arrive in San Diego with time to finish up whatever needed doing before departing in early November.

We saw what looked like a weather window and headed to Anacortes, our jumping-off point south. We had plans to travel with a buddy boat, friends on another larger Nordhavn. My brother had joined us, which meant we had three people for watches. I had no desire to attempt an overnight passage, let alone five days of them, with just us two. This is where the fears came in. Crab traps, sleeping whales, unseen fishing boats, lost-at-sea containers, lightning... We had discussed the potential hazards that faced us at night and had come up with lots to keep us on high alert 24/7.

Our friends made a snap decision to embark early, accompanying another friend down to Oregon. Our take on the weather left us unwilling to follow, so we opted to spend a few more days at home and wait for a better window. It worked – our friends ended up in Coos Bay while the storm rolled through – something they hadn't taken into account.

When we got the all-clear from our weather router we cruised out on a beautiful, calm day. First navigating west through Juan de Fuca to the Pacific Ocean, we then turned south, destination – San Francisco.

As we maneuvered past tankers and cruise ships and marvelled at the sunset that signalled the end of the day and the beginning of our first overnight, we were unsure what to expect. Although we were well equipped with electronic equipment that would allow us to 'see' what was ahead, we realized pretty quickly that in the dark we couldn't actually 'see' much of anything. Reflections from electronics' screens obscured visibility through the front window and stepping out to get a better look was a non-starter. The captain made it very clear that no one was leaving the pilothouse at night, no way, no how.

We settled into the routine… white lights turned off, red lights turned on, red plastic sheets found to cover the important equipment, towels and cushions used to cover the ones we didn't need all the time. Calm water gave way to rougher seas, as the wind picked up and the waves grew. We were being pushed from behind, but we had deployed the stabilizers (poles and fish**) long before we needed them. Now the fun began. We all started moving into our roles, I prepared a meal that we could all eat, Lawrence and my brother started the engine room checks… then my brother headed down to his bunk while Lawrence and I acclimatized ourselves to our boat at night, at sea.

Sounds seem different, have more meaning, more impact - eyes are strained trying to look into the black depths ahead of us. The radar becomes your most reliable friend, along with the screen displaying nearby AIS signals. But not everyone uses AIS. Lawrence eventually fell asleep on the settee, not comfortable enough to leave me alone (no complaints here!). There I was, scanning the instruments, using the binoculars to try to see what was ahead, marking our location on the paper chart as I made the hourly notes in the log and of course listening to the music station of my choice (country) because hey, I was in charge of EVERYTHING.

At some point there were signs of something in front of us – inconsistent blips on the radar, sporadic AIS signals… Lawrence was asleep. I needed to know. Cautiously I slid open the side door and, binoculars in hand, firmly planted one foot outside and one foot inside and leaned out to see what was up.

It was beautiful. The sky was full of stars and absolutely breathtaking. I scanned the horizon ahead (black on black) and sure enough, found a glow that aligned with where a vessel might be. It would eventually establish itself as a fishing boat (one of many we saw that night – all dead ahead). Watching the ocean pass beside us, seeing how our stabilizers sliced through the waves, and feeling the cool night air – I was mesmerized. I quickly shut the door, stepping back to my place at the helm, and settled in for the rest of my shift. A radio call to the fishing boat and confirmation of who would pass on which side left me feeling confident and more relaxed.

The moon rose, and suddenly we were cruising in soft light. Waxing full, it would illuminate our nights until San Francisco. I kept up my half-in-side-door forays during my watches, loving the comfort of seeing the sky and the sea and the stars, although I brought out my Spin-lock life vest to keep the captain happy.

One night there were dolphins, leaping through the waves and playing around the stabilizer fish**. Later, when the weather was warmer, and the side doors were open, flying fish and squid flew off the tops of the waves right into the pilothouse. I grew to enjoy the night watches, appreciating each one for its special moments (sunset, moon rise, sunrise, moon set) and found that time passed quickly. The captain started heading down to the cabin to sleep, leaving me totally alone.

When we arrived in San Francisco to a spectacular molten sunrise under the Golden Gate Bridge I was excited to catch up with our friends – but sad that I wasn't going to be back out to sea for a few days.

That quickly changed as the weather router informed us the break was smaller than we thought, and if we didn't leave right away we wouldn't leave for a week. No issues there – we left the dock the next day, happy to be heading out, more night watches, starry skies and sunrises.

Of course, this leg took us past Los Angeles, at night, with all the attendant navigational hazards that come with a huge port city. More fears… successfully faced.

Our boat could handle it – we always knew that, as the N46 Nordhavn's have more circumnavigations under their keels than most other boats around. We just weren't sure how we would do. Sitting in the saloon, looking out the back windows, I saw waves coming at us like freight trains, lifting the rounded stern of our little ship up and roaring past the side windows and she just rolled gracefully and settled back into place without complaint. The boat wasn't the issue. And as each day ended, I found that although I hadn't lost my respect and my 'on high alert' feeling as I settled into the helm seat, I truly loved the night time. We were all learning to sleep when we could, and I enjoyed keeping everyone fed (although one lamb dinner almost hit the floor when I decided to try something a bit more exciting than burritos as the seas subsided and then suddenly rose up just as I was taking the tray of chops out of the oven. Luckily it is a well-designed galley where I could wedge arms and legs into place and safely get the tray onto the counter… no harm done!).

Since that time, we have conquered the Baja Bash back to San Diego, and crossed the Sea of Cortez to Puerto Vallarta, alone. We had a lightning storm threaten for what seemed like hours, blocking our passage both out to sea and into our anchorage… frightening indeed. But we have also watched whales jump completely clear of the water as the sunrise painted everything red and gold… and enjoyed the nocturnal company of boobies who use the boat as an overnight rest stop.

Future plans? That requires some careful thought, and a new fear to face – a long distance offshore passage. But that is definitely for another day.

*An acronym for Cruise Underway to Baja Rally. A powerboat cruise from local waters to La Paz, B.C., Mexico. http://cubar.sdyc.org/

** Stabilizers used to ease the motion on an underway boat are properly called paravanes; sometimes these are nicknamed 'fish' or 'birds'.

Bio: *Northern Ranger's* Southern Adventures: We have spent years cruising, alone, with kids, with dog, and with friends – in four different boats (26 foot Tanzer Sailboat *Pagoo*; 26 foot Campion Toba powerboat and liveaboard, *Mithril*; 30 foot Campion Trawler and liveaboard and giant playpen *Pagoo*; then our first forever boat (we lied) a 43 foot North Pacific, *Malahide*; and now our new/old forever boat, a much-dreamed of and anticipated Nordhavn 46... *Nothern Ranger*. Although there are still coves to be discovered and water to be navigated up north (i.e.

ALASKA!) we made the decision to "turn left and straight on until morning"... well, lots of mornings, actually. We aren't getting any younger (says who?) and we thought that we would venture out a little further afield while the venturing was still good. The boat is more than capable of handling it, and after our journey down the coast to Mexico, we have discovered that we are more than capable too. (No accident, that – we have been preparing for this for years!)

So now, with the boat several air-plane rides away, we wait with baited breath for that magical thing called "retirement". I retired years ago (out of the frying pan and into the fire, as in, full time housewife and everything that goes with that! Fun!) but the other half and titular Captain of the ship still needs to show up once in a while to prove that he is still working for The Company.

We read with envy the blogs and letters from cruisers who cast off and drift away for years and years and years... and hopefully one day in the not-too-distant-future, that will be us. But meanwhile! Long plane rides and short excursions are in our plans. And really, there's absolutely nothing wrong with that. Baby steps!

northernrangeradventures.com

21

Taking the Plunge

by Brianna Snider

The moment had come, my heart was racing and trying to make its way out of my chest.

Fear enveloped my mind like a cocoon as I lay there floating on top of the icy water of the Pacific Ocean in my wet suit, mask, snorkel, and tank; about to venture to the bottom on my very first ocean dive. It was much more than I could have imagined, away from the safety of the four walls of the pool. It was a completely different feeling to when we practiced in the pool. I no longer felt safe, I didn't know what was down there, or if something was lurking in the shadows waiting for its prey to come by so it could have lunch.

As the water slowly swept over my head and I started my descent, I felt like I was going to be sick, I needed a way out. My instructor and classmates all dove down at the same time to the bottom, about 30 feet down, and then there was me, hyperventilating into my mask and snorkel barely keeping it together.

About half way down, I couldn't take it anymore. I quickly did what we were instructed to do in case of emergency, I threw my hand up in the air, screamed, and kicked as hard as I could until I reached the surface again and returned to safety.

I grabbed my mask off my face and took one long hard gulp of air. I was safe again. Safe, but alone on the surface of the choppy water. It was a few minutes until my instructor resurfaced to make sure I was ok. I calmed down for a moment and he asked if I wanted to try submerging again. I needed to get my bearings, I needed to prepare myself.

I can do this, I thought to myself.

'Take it slow, and try and relax,' my instructor Tony insisted.

Ok, here I go. This isn't scary, everyone else can do this, you can too. I gave myself a quick pep talk before attempting to dive down again.

The water slowly swallowed me again as I made my way down towards the others at the bottom of the ocean. I was having such mixed emotions, it was neat but weird to be able to see as far out into the deeper waters off Ogden Point in Victoria. I felt like a tiny ant in a vast but also majestic world. It was truly a new world that not many have truly explored or even had the ability or desire to do so. I felt at peace.

A school of fish swam past me in a hurry and I could feel every flutter of their tiny fins hitting my wet suit and exposed hands. I really felt like I was right in the middle of a mermaid's playground. It was almost indescribable. My instructor Tony picked up a very large purple sun star from the bottom and turned it upside down as he tried to place it on my head. I wasn't having it and swam away in fright. My friend Ally, on the other hand, stayed in place as he placed the sun star on her head. It looked like she was wearing a wig, Mother Nature at its finest.

Moments later, I was facing Ally and she was facing me near the bottom pointing at something for me to look at. I took one look behind her and saw an enormous black fish almost the same size as Ally coming up right behind her. I motioned to her to look behind her, and the look of terror on her face through her SCUBA mask was like no other. The fish swam off and was of no threat to us, but it was daunting and a little bit terrifying just the same. In the wild, you never know if something bigger than you will try to eat you.

The vibrant colors and creatures that we found below the surface were spectacular. The oranges, purples, pinks, reds, greens, and browns were magnified in the water. It would have been a shame to miss this opportunity to experience something different, and to not brave the unknown to have the experience of a lifetime seemed downright scandalous. I didn't know what I was so afraid of before. The unknown is frightening, and a place that one must overcome to be free and be able to enjoy life.

Our time was all but up and we all began to resurface. After an underwater show of a lifetime, I decided I wouldn't let fear stand in my way again. We resurfaced and headed back to shore. I didn't realize how tired you become from diving, I barely had enough energy to swim the two hundred metres back to the beach. My body was exhausted; mentally, emotionally, and physically. A hot shower and rest beckoned.

After that first dive, I dove more and more, each dive becoming easier than my first. I felt a little silly after having a full-blown panic attack under water, but you never know how your body, or your mind will react to new experiences. I persevered, moved past my fears and triumphed over my anxiety. I am so thankful that on that day I faced my fears and finally took the plunge.

Bio: Brianna Snider is currently working for the Canadian Coast Guard as a Project Officer with Environmental Response. From the time she was a new-born living on a sailboat, to the time she now spends in the office looking out onto the water, her love of the ocean has taken her many places. She has seen many sunrises and sunsets across the ocean and up the coast of beautiful British Columbia during her time spent as a deckhand for the Coast Guard. Now working ashore, she has a loving husband and two kids who are her pride and joy. Her hobbies are camping, hiking, writing, laughing, spending time with her kids and being an advocate for women in non-traditional roles.
Even though she doesn't go to sea anymore, she still loves the smell of the salty sea air and she will always be a sailor at heart. Brianna lives with her husband and two kids in Victoria, B.C
www.womenatsea.ca

22

The Risk Averse Sailor

by Brita Marie Siepker

I'm the kind of girl who must summit every mountain she approaches, and never stays in one place long enough for moss to grow under her. But I'm also the kind of girl who wears her seatbelt in the backseat of a car and her helmet on a bicycle. I am about as risk averse as an adventurous wanderluster can be.

How does a risk averse sailor cast off the bowlines and sail across oceans?

The Risk Averse Sailor only sails on seaworthy vessels – vessels that can handle more than she can, vessels that will keep her safe when she's down and out. She likes full keels, center cockpits, and stainless lifelines. She doesn't sail during hurricane or cyclone season; she doesn't set out on a passage when a storm is predicted; she only sets sails when conditions are forecasted to be manageable for the vessel she's on and the crew she's with; and she sails away from weather that brews up while she's at sea. The Risk Averse Sailor keeps her vessel well maintained, well fueled, and full of extra food and water.

The Risk Averse Sailor reefs early and shakes out reefs late. She drops the traveler before the toe rail goes under and shortens sail before the autohelm allows the bow to round up. She vigilantly watches clouds on the horizon and splotches on the radar, ready to furl or heave-to if bad weather approaches. She sails in wind she's comfortable with – 15-20 knots on a light day cruiser, 25-30 knots on a heavy ocean cruiser – and if it kicks up any higher she requests help from her crew to keep the boat under control. The Risk Averse Sailor does not let schedules or competition dictate her course or speed.

The Risk Averse Sailor studies the International Regulations for Preventing Collisions at Sea, the rules on conduct of vessels, navigation lights, sound and light signals, aids to navigation, and charts. She obeys the rules, even where there isn't another boat in hundreds of miles to see her navigational lights, even when a cut corner might be more expeditious and still likely safe. She doesn't assume other vessels know the rules, and, in the case of charter boats and boats underway with fenders in the water, assumes they don't. In all cases, she steers a wide berth of other vessels and goes the extra distance to find the deeper water. The Risk Averse Sailor knows the rules, follows the rules, and makes room for those that don't.

The Risk Averse Sailor has two rules: (1) Stay on the boat, and (2) Don't hit anything.

The Risk Averse Sailor never leaves the cockpit without a PFD buckled on and an EPIRB and strobe light zipped into the PFD. If the conditions are bad or it's night time, she only leaves the cockpit with a tether clipped between her PFD and the jacklines running up and down the deck. She always follows the adage, 'One hand for the boat, one hand for you,' holding onto lifelines and eyebrows and stations and shrouds as she makes her way forward and aft. She wraps an arm around the furled sail when she perches up on the bow pulpit to watch for bommies. The Risk Averse Sailor practices man overboard drills and mentally prepares for one anytime a crew goes forward in difficult conditions. The Risk Averse Sailor never approaches anything at a faster speed than she's willing to hit it at. She approaches all docks, mooring balls and anchorages at a slow enough speed to not need reverse to stop forward motion. If the depth shoals unexpectedly or another vessel approaches closely, she backs off on speed to assess the situation. The Risk Averse Sailor believes that slow is pro, and doesn't let her crew's impatience hurry her.

The Risk Averse Sailor isn't afraid to stay in harbor when conditions require it, but usually feels safer at sea, far from the hazards of land. The Risk Averse Sailor would always rather be at sea than on land, so analyze those risks, take those precautions and cast off those bowlines!

Bio: Brita Siepker learned to sail at the Manhattan Yacht Club in New York. She has been cruising full time since January 2015 and is currently circumnavigating with the World Arc 2018/2019. You can follow her adventures at www.lifeiswater.com.

23

Bermuda to Azores – A Whale of a Tale

by Sheri Hunt

We were more than 1,200 nautical miles across the Atlantic, enjoying a calm sunny morning, when suddenly, something shook the boat. We were stunned. We hit something...We *must* have hit something. *But out here? In the middle of the Atlantic? What did we hit?* Then, BOOM! It happened again. An object was careening down the port side surrounded by a brownish red oily slick. *Was it the jagged corner of a container?* The whole of our stern wake was now a sickly dark color. We frantically searched for answers and wondered what the fate of our boat and the four souls onboard would be.

Seven days previously we had set off from St George, Bermuda. We departed from St George just after 1500 hours, delayed as we waited for a series of storm cells to pass by. That is one of my worst fears in a boat on the water. With an 88-foot carbon mast rising higher into the afternoon sky than many of the trees on the banks of the beautiful harbor I thought that staying in the harbor seemed to be a safer haven than alone out on the dark teal, dangerous, Bermuda reef waters under black ominous thunderheads. Using every tool that I had onboard, along with local information, we determined that we had a 12-hour window to get out of the harbor and offshore into a beautiful south westerly breeze. A breeze that should easily carry us north east to catch a current and steady breeze towards the Azores. So, waiting a couple hours was the right thing to do. My crew were ready to go as soon as we cleared-out with customs.

This was to be a first Atlantic Ocean crossing for all of us. While I have more than 15,000 sea miles sailing in the Pacific Ocean, and having completed the Newport to Bermuda sailboat race, this was my first time going east of Bermuda. This would also be the longest time at sea for me on my newest boat. I had three crew joining with fantastic coastal racer experience whom had also never sailed the Atlantic. I was feeling more apprehension than usual, although confident in our seamanship and the newly refitted S&S 58-foot Northwind yacht. The time to leave had arrived and we pushed off the customs dock, hoisted the main to the first reef point, and motored out through the cut.

The new 4G radar worked perfectly, guiding us through the remaining rain cells as the sun was setting. The flashes of lightning in the black clouds on the horizon gave us an amazing show, especially since we witnessed it from afar. We were off and settling into our first night watch. We worked in pairs on short watch rotations, although the boat was expertly driven by the new NKE instruments and autopilot. The 12-14 knot breeze (True Wind Angle (TWA) 145) on the 155 percent headsail and reefed mainsail was very comfortable as we made 7 knots of boat speed. The bonus of a TWA solution for driving with the autopilot downwind helped ease everyone into their night watches. I stole a couple of hours of rest that first night which surprised me. The initial fears eased as we sorted out some of the nuances of offshore sailing.

After 800 miles at sea we were all feeling quite comfortable with the passage. All systems were performing as expected. We were receiving weather on demand from the Pactor modem with SSB* Radio set-up and sending stories home daily to family and friends. All the routing software was indicating the next four days to be mild when I was informed that the water from the water tanks was 'tannish' in color as it ran out of the tap. One thousand miles to go. With four people aboard and a nightmare no-one ever wants to address at sea: this had just become a reality. More than 250 gallons of water aboard may not be fit for drinking.

After I stopped fighting myself internally, I set about checking the water quality and the water making system. Total solids were a bit high for my RO watermaker but superior to any bottled drinking water on the market. The pH was neutral. The water tasted fine (to me). But it was obviously a tan color when run into a white container from the tanks. The only solution I could find for a short-term fix was to disconnect the output from the watermaker and to fill plastic jugs daily to minimize storage. This satisfied everyone aboard and remained the water protocol for the rest of the passage.

Another 400 miles flew by as we had champagne sailing conditions with our best 24-hour run equalling 220 nautical miles! A true testament to the crew's ability to keep the boat moving. We saw a maximum speed of just over 12 knots on one of the watches. Every day we witnessed an amazing number of turtles, flying fish, and dolphins. The speeds were perfect for the bow riders to demonstrate their superb athleticism as they raced in and around us day and night under the brilliant sunshine and a waxing moon. As the days passed we noticed the waters were filling with more and more Portuguese man-of-wars as the winds softened and finally abandoned us, leaving us making 4 knots on 'lake' Atlantic Ocean. We were just on the edge of the Azores High even though we were still 600 nm from Faial Island.

It was just after the change of the morning watch in these light-wind sailing conditions when suddenly the boat lurched and there was a loud smashing sound of hitting something. Then within seconds of the first concussion there was a second, less physical, but just as loud collision sound. I was on the stern and rose to see an object careening down the port side surrounded by a brownish red oily slick. I saw what looked like the jagged corner of a container. I spoke to the watchperson that I thought we had hit a container.

'Note the latitude and longitude and hand-steer the helm,' I said. In the next moment, I turned to see if anything reappeared behind the boat, when I saw the bottom jaw of a toothed whale rise out of the water. The whale disappeared once again into the reddish slick and then reappeared as a large pectoral fin rose out of the water rolling the whale over while diving. A good sign for the whale.

Now to check out how the boat had fared.

The crew were all on deck now. I called on two of the crew to do a bilge check, bow to stern, and check the keel bolts. The helmsman was asked to assess the rudder and steering for changes. I issued a PAN-PAN on the radio. A nearby boat, ahead of us by about 20 nm, responded and stated they would stand by with sails down until we could determine whether we were okay or if assistance was needed. I also called on the satellite phone to my land-based emergency crew and relayed the circumstances. Their initial response was that we had struck a whale and that the whale had 'tail slapped' us resulting in the two collision sounds.

After a nerve wracking 45 minutes we completed the checks aside from going into the water to assess underwater damage. I radioed back to the ship on standby and let them know we had determined that if there was damage it was not significant enough to warrant their help, (although I did take down their SSB channel information, so I could join them later should something change.)

The next 24-hours for me were the hardest of my life. Every creek or groan that the boat made turned my stomach and had me fearing for a significant change in the circumstances, but none came. The waters remained flat and then we becalmed, requiring us to motor. Around 0200 the watch crew noticed a strange jingling sound and hesitation from the engine. I rolled out of my bunk, foggy headed, and yet so pleased to be sailing with such capable crew. I spent the next half hour in the engine compartment checking fluids and tightening belts while we drifted quietly in the middle of the Atlantic Ocean under a bright full moon. Fearless adventurers finding our way across the ocean.

With 2,000 nm behind us we arrived in Horta City, Faial Island in the Azores at sunrise, escorted by an early morning pilot whale. It was time for some well-earned relaxation and we were just in time for the Wimbledon tennis final, which was enjoyed in Peter's Café Sport of course! Then on to attending to the boat's recovery needs and painting the breakwater with our flag. The trip had thrown plenty of challenges and fear at us all but had been an unforgettable and rewarding adventure.

*Single-Sideband

Bio: Captain Sheri holds a USCG 50 ton with auxiliary sail license. She is an avid offshore racer and has participated in the TransPac race from Los Angeles to Hawaii multiple times finishing just off overall podium in 2013 as navigator, however winning the honor of first amateur boat to finish. In addition, she is a PADI certified Dive Master. A member of the 1991 World Championship-winning USA women's rugby team, she has recently been inducted into the American Rugby Hall of Fame.

www.SV-Nanami.com
https://www.patreon.com/ExperienceNanami

24

Kuaka

by Mo FitzPatrick

My grandfather was a sailor, my father was sailor, and I was a girl who wanted to be a sailor. My dad told a good yarn, anecdotes of adventurous achievements that entertained my brother but spun a web of fear around my ten-year-old self.

My grandfather took his girlfriend sailing and capsized the boat, throwing them both ashore on a little rocky island. She forgave him, married him, and produced my dad. My dad took his friend sailing, capsized the boat and was rescued by the French Navy. They got their picture in the paper. I went sailing and was scared to capsize.

I learned to sail on the Tamaki River in New Zealand. It was a beautiful place and an exciting one for a young girl. On the far side of the river the land was flat, but on the boat club side sandstone cliffs guarded the water's edge. A steep track cut through the cliffs, led down to a series of little beaches and reefs. Ancient pohutukawa trees, evolved to survive in salt water, grew out of the cliffs, providing cool shade and the most excellent rope swings. On club days I had as much fun on the beach as on the water.

My older brother raced a P Class, quite successfully, and I would float around in an Optimist until the rescue boat came and towed me in. My mum worked in the galley, cooking sausages and supplying cups of tea to wet and cold sailors. In the mornings my dad helped with rigging, launching, and retrieving the boats. In the afternoons he sailed with my brother in one of the club Arrows. The Arrow was known as a 'Father and Son' yacht, a discriminatory designation that pleased my brother and annoyed me.

I enjoyed sailing except for three things. I hated the puffy orange lifejacket with the big collar that I had to wear. It was uncomfortable, and I looked like a little pumpkin in it. I hated that every lesson finished with a race and I was always last because I had no idea what I was doing. And I hated the thought of capsizing.

Every sailing course includes a capsize lesson. With my family history I thought that capsizing would come naturally if for some reason I needed to do it. I didn't see it as a necessary skill to learn. I don't know exactly what I was scared of. *Knocking my head? Falling into the water? Being trapped under the sail?* The only time I wanted to be upside down was on the rope swing and I think the reason I was always last in the races was because I was concentrating on keeping the boat upright.

When we had to capsize I climbed out of the boat into the water. But I left the mainsheet jammed in the cleat and the boat sailed away from me. The Optimist was sailing better than it ever had before, and for a while the adults in the rescue boat didn't realise I wasn't aboard. In my puffy lifejacket there was no way that I could swim after my boat, so I just tried not to get run over.

Then one unforgettable day something happened that cut the threads of my fear. Dad had another yarn to tell and I had a place in the family sailing lore. It was early in spring and my brother, for some reason, couldn't sail. My dad needed a crew in the 'Father and Son' race. I went sailing with my dad in the Arrow. Father and Daughter. The day was chilly with gusts of wind blipping over the water and I wore two jerseys. We rigged the boat on the beach then Dad checked my lifejacket and we pushed the boat into the water. He told me to jump in and take the tiller. My nerves were flapping like a luffing sail, but his voice was reassuring and gave me confidence.

We sat side-by-side on the gunwale and it didn't feel like we would tip over. Dad gave me only a few simple instructions and lots of encouragement. I pointed the boat where he told me and kept us steady. Meanwhile Dad adjusted the jib sheet and the mainsheet. We tacked and tacked, and I thought it was all practice. I was concentrating so hard I didn't realise the race had started.

Dad was sitting in front of me and after a while I relaxed enough to look at him. He had a massive grin on his face. Then he started talking. He told me stories about the Tamaki River. In the old days the river was an important waterway for the Maori. When his father was a boy the Maori still paddled their mighty waka between the two harbours of the

Manukau and the Waitemata. Then he told me about the godwit, which the Maori call kuaka.

The kuaka is a wading bird that feeds and breeds in the Arctic summer. Every year they migrate, flying thousands of miles to arrive in New Zealand in spring. When they get here the birds are hungry and skinny but soon they fatten up, feeding on the mudflats like those of the Tamaki River. Then in autumn they leave New Zealand and return to the Arctic. Dad pointed to the opposite shore. I could see the kuaka, some on the ground and some in the air. I was sure the ones flying were just finishing their mega mile journey.

Then Dad said, 'Imagine it. The kuaka leaves the safety of the shore and flies over the ocean. It must be a determined bird. It has to believe that it will get to New Zealand. What an adventure.' Then Dad turned to me and added, 'You know, for the kuaka success is getting to the finish. It doesn't matter if it is first or last.' I could see the admiration in my dad's eyes and I decided that I wanted to be like the kuaka. I wanted to be brave and fly an unwavering course.

I don't know if it was his words or what happened next but after that day I was no longer worried about coming last and I was no longer afraid to capsize. I can't remember where we came in that race. But we crossed the finish line. And then we capsized. Suddenly I was in the water and, except that it was freezing cold, I was ok. I wondered why the kuaka didn't stop somewhere warm on their migration. The Arrow had turned turtle and the top of the mast was stuck in the mud. It took a lot of effort getting the boat back upright.

Mum had a hot cup of tea waiting for us. She had watched the capsize from the clubhouse. She saw me swimming around, shivering and determined, and she saw Dad standing on the bottom. I was a bit mad when I found this out but then she called him *Limosa* which is the Latin name for the kuaka and means muddy.

That night my brother asked where we came in the race and I told him that we got to the finish. Dad said, 'It was a successful race,' which annoyed my brother and pleased me because I knew what he meant.

Bio: At 12-years old Mo wrote her first story about a kid who ran away to sea. Another 12 years on and Mo realised her dream – a 4,000 nm journey across the Pacific. Mo lives on the yacht *Sam* with her partner Danny and enjoys sailing and diving.

25

Struck by a Sumatra

by Deb Bott

Fear, according to the English Oxford Dictionary, has a few meanings, one of those is as a noun and states: 'An unpleasant emotion caused by the threat of danger, pain, or harm.' Facing your fear is not something a sailor does on purpose. If anything, we go to extreme lengths to avoid situations where we will be forced to face our fears. However, Mother Nature challenges that.

While sailing, I fear storms. Specifically, the 'Sumatras' of South East Asia. These occur during the south west monsoon season, from April to November. They bring strong winds, come in fast and are very nasty. Their name is due to their origin, as they emanate from the mountains of Sumatra. Sumatras are a collection of thunderstorms which merge creating one powerful cell while moving towards the west coasts of Malaysia, Singapore, and Borneo. Their impending arrival can be seen as a squall line, a long definitive line of dark cloud, with a white top.

During the month of July 2017, we anchored in a picturesque bay at Pulau Temaju, a small island off the west coast of West Kalimantan, Borneo, Indonesia. As we entered the bay, we noticed many bamboo fishing houses, not unusual for this region. However, all of them seemed to be broken. We thought that maybe the village had moved on and had left these fishing houses to decay, also not unusual for this area. It made for an interesting trip into the bay because as these bamboo structures decay, they leave bamboo stumps in the ground, protruding at water level at different angles. In essence, they become spears.

As we approached Pulau Temaju, we checked and rechecked every single medium of weather available so as to gauge the evening's wind, and low winds were forecast. The anchorage was reasonably well protected from the south west. All seemed well, so in we went and dropped our anchor. Our afternoon could not have been more perfect, we had the bay entirely to ourselves. The water was turquoise, and the beach fringed with white sand and coconut trees; completing our vision of paradise. It was like a postcard. However, by 2130 all hell had broken loose.

During the afternoon a local fisherman called by, neither of us could speak the other's language, but this didn't stop us all having a laugh. We gave him some fishing gear and in turn he gave us fish. During our conversation with the fisherman, he pointed to the water and shook his head, 'no', we both nodded saying, 'Oh that's no good, no fish here'.

We spent the rest of the afternoon swimming, reading, and relaxing in awe of our idyllic surroundings, musing at the others who had pushed on into the south easterly to the Pontianak River.

What a shame they will miss out on such a find, we thought, How lucky are we to have it all to ourselves!

That night we cooked up a feast, enjoying a few beers, and watched a movie. We were settled on the settee when we noticed it had started to rain. We got up to shut hatches and without a word of a lie, the wind went from a gentle 4-6 knots from the south (coming directly over the land) to 42-46 knots directly from the west within 10 minutes.

We couldn't believe how quickly the waves and swell had formed. We hoped that like most Sumatras we had experienced, this one would only last about an hour, then pass as if nothing had happened. The night sky was lit up constantly with lightning strikes, as if to show off the three massive squall lines approaching; the sight was daunting.

On previous occasions, if we saw a Sumatra approaching we would quickly haul anchor and move *Matilda* to a protected anchorage. This was not feasible this time, it had come in too fast. The conditions had quickly turned violent, so we decided to start our engine to ease the tension on the anchor and chain.

I retreated below because the conditions outside were frightening, my adrenaline was pumping, and I had the shakes. To distract myself, I turned on our navigation PC, which has open CPN installed, this way I could see our track out of the anchorage if need be. Thank heavens we keep our tracks every single time we move. I also tightened the circle on our GPS drag alarm. I was yelling out to Bruce, at the helm, the wind strength, depth and if we were drifting – we were not.

Inside *Matilda* it was now hot, pitching and rolling horribly as the surf smashed into our starboard side. The motion inside was revolting. I couldn't go outside at all, I was frightened to the point of being paralysed. My ultimate fear was happening right now. In the seven years we had owned *Matilda*, I had never vomited from seasickness until this night. I was feeling wretched, terrified and faint all at the same time. However, I was fully aware of what Bruce was going through and I felt dreadful being so out of control and useless. Through the chaos he realised I was vomiting so he laid me down on the settee, covered me with a blanket, put the fans on me, put my bucket beside me, and told me to not move. I didn't. I couldn't.

As I was watching him, I realised what an amazing man he is. His calmness always surprises me when I least expect it. As I was laying there vomiting, feeling dreadful and overwhelmed with everything happening around me, I heard the chain running out at a very fast rate from the chain locker. I screamed to Bruce, 'The chain is deploying itself!'. I ran out, took the helm and he went to the bow. In the mad rush I'd forgotten about vomiting and left the bucket behind.

It was the first time I had been outside for about 30 minutes and it was like a nightmare. The wind was roaring, the swell was well established and white water was rushing over the starboard side and into our cockpit. The aggressive rolling and pitching of our floating home was extremely frightening. Bruce was at the bow to stop the chain from deploying itself, I thought then he should have clipped on but in the chaos, we didn't even think about it.

I don't think I took a breath as I looked towards the bow, watching it disappear underwater. So violent was the motion, Bruce had to crawl on hands and knees around the pulpit.

Unbelievably he stopped the chain from running out, he then crawled back to the cockpit to me. Only then did I remember to keep breathing. He looked at me and said, 'We have a slight problem, the snubber has melted, and the backup snubber has parted, so we need to move, or we are going to rip the winch from the deck.' Only then did I remember my bucket!

At this stage I couldn't cope with anything at all. Bruce was calm and gave me explicit instructions on how we were going to haul the anchor and move *Matilda* out of the anchorage. I couldn't believe we had to do this. Once again, he crawled forward, I followed his hand signals and we did it. The sight of him disappearing as the bow was submerged is etched in my mind. I was terrified of losing him.

Once he was back in the cockpit he unselfishly instructed me to go back to the settee and lie back down. I was a mess and no good to him. I have never experienced anything like this in my life. I was terrified.

I fell asleep on the settee, only to be woken by Bruce asking me to come out and let him know if I felt we were too close to the fisherman. I started crying at the sight of fishing boats very close to us and said, 'Yes sweetheart we are.' We were so close we could have handed them a drink, so we moved *Matilda*.

On reflection, even if the overall forecast has no west in it, don't expose yourself to the west in the south west monsoon season. Next time a fisherman is pointing to the water and shaking his head 'no', this may mean 'this place is no good – move', and if the bamboo fishing houses are in tatters, this could be an indicator the bay gets hammered in foul weather.

Bruce had moved *Matilda* out of the anchorage, past all the spears and to the safety of the lee of the island. *Matilda* was in calm water with more than 30 fishing boats. We wondered if our earlier visitor had watched us come into the protected side of Palau Temaju.

My story has a double ending. I had also faced in real time, the fear of losing Bruce. A fear I never, ever want to face again.

Bio: Deb and her partner Bruce have been liveaboards since 2010 and have been full-time cruisers along Australia's east coast since 2014. Deb has been sailing Queensland's Moreton Bay and the Great Sandy Straits since 2005 starting out in a 20-foot trailer-sailor, then a 30-foot Beneteau and now living on board their 43-foot Hans Christian-Christina *Matilda*, currently sailing SE Asia. Receive monthly newsletters and keep up to date by following their blog: www.svmatilda.com

26

Petraphobia

by Mikayla-Rose Brumby

Eucalyptus... The most amazing smell when one has just crossed Bass Straight and hasn't seen or smelt land for more than three days. Oils wafted through the air and we breathed it in like drinking fresh cool water after days in a parched desert.

We arrived at Refuge Cove, Victoria, at 0530 just as daylight broke and were dismayed at our discovery. With no need for using the motor, as we had enjoyed fair winds, we were confused when we turned on the starboard motor and didn't move. Using the port engine, we motored into the cove, this was rather tricky as we have a fairly big boat and when you're manoeuvring amongst others with only one motor it becomes difficult! We dropped anchor and my two brothers leapt into the freezing water to have a look at the motor. They emerged shivering with the verdict: unpleasant news that created a dilemma... We had no propeller!

The crew assembled for a meeting and we all sat down with suggestions. Firstly, we became excited when we discovered TWO spare props! But, no fixing nut to hold either of them on. We decided to set off straight away to head to Franklin Harbour so that we could obtain a replacement. If we wanted to beat the bad weather that was headed our way, we had to leave immediately. We hurriedly pulled up anchor and started the port engine.

As we neared the heads, we noticed a strange sound. Leaning over the edge I detected more bad news, there was no water coming out the side - this meant that the engine could overheat as the cooling system was not working. Uh-Oh! The engine was cut, and we ditched the anchor once again.

Now we had a huge problem, we were stranded between the heads with NO WORKING ENGINES! High swell was rolling in and we were all feeling seasick. Stress levels were high, and I bit my lip in fear. Mater ducked into the engine bay to find out what was going wrong, he soon located a shredded v-belt.

We were very aware of a storm approaching rapidly. Fear tingled down my spine.

Mum and I jumped in the two showers to cool down the engines. As we struggled to keep our feet in the shower, Mum at least enjoyed nice steamy warm water, whilst on the other side of the boat, I suffered icy temperatures.

By the time we emerged from our contrasting showers Mater had hit the sack exhausted from doing night-shift previously and tinkering around in the engine bay, the Captain had sputtered along with a sick engine, and we were finally feeling protected and safe in the bay. Dad dug around trying to find a spare v-belt.

After a while he realized that it was under Mater's bed so waking Mater up we extracted it and got it sorted. Because we had taken so long trying to locate it and finally putting the belt on, we had lost precious time. It would now be too risky to sail to Franklin Harbour before the storm set in.

Instead we decided to anchor overnight. Lisa cooked up a delicious tuna mornay, which we relished, for tea. After surviving on crackers for the last few days due to high seas and seasickness, our meal was incredible. Once restored the whole crew rowed the tender to shore. Savouring the feeling of our feet on terra firma, we could have kissed the ground with relief.

That night we retired to bed early and rose with the sun ready to begin our day of repairs. I had found a leak in my bedroom which meant my mattress was soaked in one corner, the kitchen door had fallen off, and we had to double check engines.

With the majority of the repairs fixed (or temporarily sorted) we still had a few hours of daylight remaining. Lisa and I went crabbing whilst Robert and Mater enjoyed spear fishing, leaving Mum and Dad to tend to the boat.

That evening whilst lounging on the front netting, enjoying small nibbles of crab and feasting on delicious fresh fish the boys had caught, we became aware of an unusual sensation. The evening air was eerie. The sunset was beautiful, but nothing felt right.

Wind would blow through our hair with a hot gust and then quite suddenly turn icy cold, biting our cheeks. We huddled on the deck wrapped in towels to keep us warm, constantly throwing them off from the heat and then snuggling back into it as the next cold bite flew in. The south wind was howling, bringing in cold air from Antarctica, then it would catch the hot air from land and swirl it, creating a motion like a whirlwind. It swirled around the open area where we were anchored.

We decided to stay another night and settled down contentedly with our tummies bulging, to hopefully have a peaceful night of rest after a long week of night sailing from Sydney. We knew we still had to go to get to Adelaide, so we snuggled down in satisfaction.

The night was tranquil to me but not to Mum and Dad who kept waking as other boats around us pulled up anchor and then re-anchored in a slightly different place as they kept dragging.

The serenity of the night was broken by screams.

'ROCKS! OH, MY GOODNESS ROCKS!' Screamed my mother hysterically. 'OH MY GOODNESS! WE'RE GOING TO HIT THE ROCKS!' She screamed and screamed until everyone on board had leapt from their toasty warm beds and out into the icy cold night air.

The evening went from entirely silent except the lapping of the waves, to the wind whistling through the ropes and terror. Sounds filled the air; voices yelling and screaming, electronics beeping, engine roaring, torches clicking on. The crew slipped and slid on the dewy deck as they tried to see exactly what was going on.

Rocks, just like my mother had screamed, only two metres away!

The wind was swirling like it had been earlier but much more ferocious. Because of this circular motion the anchor had worked its way loose and we were in a panic!

It was around three o'clock in the morning and everyone had been asleep. Mum had woken up with a strange feeling, 'As though an angel had shoved me out of bed,' she told us later. She sleepily walked out of her cabin and pulled herself up the stairs, she slid the door open as quietly as she could and stepped outside, shining her torch around in an arc she immediately was screaming, 'OH MY GOODNESS! ROCKS!' Just like a banshee, Mater complained later, but boy were we glad she had screamed that loud, otherwise that would've been our last sailing trip on our beautiful catamaran, *Selah.*

'Cut the anchor!' yelled Dad acting quite the captain. Robert brought out the machete and hacked the rope in one swift motion. The rope drifted away and with it, our spare anchor. We still had our main anchor that Mater was hurriedly pulling up. Mum was still on torch duty, swinging it around lighting up the rocks that were far too close for comfort. Everyone was freezing cold, clad in pyjamas, no jackets on to keep us warm. We shivered as we shouted directions and relayed instructions to each other. Working as a team we finally dropped the anchor again where we thought we were safe. In relief we all collapsed, damp from the salty spray of the sea, into our beds. All except Mum, who plonked down at the kitchen table and read one of my books to keep herself awake. There was no way Mum was going to relax after our fearful experience, she sat up on watch until daybreak.

In the morning, our land crew who were in Adelaide reported that the Spirit of Tasmania (car ferry) had broken free from its moorings the same night. We weren't alone in having difficulties with the wind!

Fortunately, we retrieved our anchor when Robert and Mater went snorkelling to locate it. This made us feel extremely blessed as anchors are expensive and with our new boat there had already been high costs. Who knew what else would happen as we travelled our vessel homewards.

We cleaned up after our night's adventure, and early in the morning we set sail heading into the sunrise with 4 metre swells greeting us. Port Fairy here we come… I sighed with relief as the fear of hitting rocks subsided and we made our way out to sea.

Bio: My name is Mikayla Brumby, I'm 15 years old. We own a catamaran and I have been sailing since I was five. My interests include reading books, writing novels, dancing, photography and of course; sailing.

https://selahsailingwordpresscom.wordpress.com/

27

Once is Enough

by Janet Erken

A note from the Editors:

David Heath sent us this entry with this message:

'Will a posthumous work do? Janet was my soulmate for over 32 years, but she died in 2013 of Ovarian Cancer. We built our 38ft cutter and sailed over halfway around the World.

This was published back in 1977 or 78. It occurred in the Fall of 1977 as we began our two-year trip from Seattle to Acapulco, Tahiti, Hawaii, British Columbia, Canada, and we returned to Seattle in the late Summer of 1979.'

David imparted the following advice for others going through tough times, 'For me, there were many things that helped, but, the most important was a quote by Dr. Seuss, "Do not cry because it is over. Smile because it happened."'

Janet's story:

All of us, I think, believe ourselves to be somewhat immortal and, therefore, tend to feel we're strong, fairly surefooted, and certainly not going to fall off our boats. Well, I have been swept overboard... and once is enough

We were sailing south, down the coast of California about five miles offshore. It was a glorious day, a nice following wind most of the day and we planned to anchor at San Simeon. At about five in the afternoon, the fog rolled in. We decided we couldn't possibly find San Simeon in the fog because there is only a lighted buoy there.

However, about six miles north of San Simeon is Piedras Blancas, where there is a buoy with a fog horn, a lighthouse, and a radio beacon.

There was no proper chart, but the US Coast Pilot talked about a good anchorage just to the south of the lighthouse. That seemed to be the logical anchorage to try to find in the fog.

We found the buoy by zeroing in on the radio beacon. The buoy sits about a mile and a half south west of the lighthouse. From there we bagged the sails, started the engine, and headed on a bearing toward the lighthouse with the idea that if we didn't see it in a mile we'd turn back. At a mile, we still hadn't seen the lighthouse, but it was still 280 feet deep so we continued slowly, inching our way north east.

About a quarter of a mile later we saw the light, but at that same moment we saw breakers ahead. One crewman was below calling out the depths: 80 feet – 50 feet – 30 feet – 15 feet – 7 feet – all in a space of about five seconds. The helm was hard-over, we were in reverse trying to turn and from the starboard beam we saw an enormous breaker! My first thought was, *My God, it's all over.* The next awareness I had was rolling through the breaker and wondering if I could hold my breath long enough to surface. Obviously, I did and when I surfaced I saw the boat still afloat, mast and all, about 30 yards away. At the time, I was wearing a pair of jeans, warm-up pants, foul weather boots, two pair of wool socks, a t-shirt, two wool sweaters, a fiber filled jacket, and a foul weather rain jacket. Needless to say, swimming was difficult.

I called out for help, not knowing if anyone was left on board to help. Then I remembered I had a flash-light in my pocket. But when I turned it on it didn't work. I thought that I was going to die and my parents would be so upset! I began yelling with renewed vigor. After a few moments the flashlight began to work, and that is how the crew was able to locate me. I had a flotation device in my pocket which was supposed to inflate when it got wet. It did just that but had no place to expand in the pocket, so it popped. However, I wasn't aware of that. My jacket had some air trapped in it and it did give me some buoyancy. I discovered I was in a kelp patch and my legs were becoming entangled in it as I was treading water.

Meanwhile back on the boat, everyone else was still on board. Below decks was wet and a shambles, the floorboards were just awash, but the hull wasn't leaking. They anchored immediately and began bailing. When noses were counted and they discovered I was gone, one crew member jumped in the water with two life jackets to swim out to me... and out again as it was so cold he couldn't even catch his breath. He realized there were no breakers between me and the boat, so he put the dinghy in the water. After discovering one oar had been broken, he sculled the dinghy out to me.

By now I had been in the water about ten minutes. I was exhausted, and I realized I couldn't save myself by swimming the 100 yards to the boat. Needless to say, I was terrified. I had strange thoughts, *Why isn't my life flashing before my eyes? I've lost my ring. If this is really the end make it fast, I'm so exhausted.*

Suddenly I heard one of the crew yelling to me to hang on, help was on the way. Oh God, what a relief. When he arrived I just hung onto the transom and rested. Becoming aware of the breakers and the terrifying sound they were making, I kept looking over my shoulder to see if one was going to break over me. After resting a few moments, I tried to pull myself into the dinghy but couldn't. Normally I weigh about 115 pounds but with all that wet clothing I must have weighed 200 pounds. Finally, I was pulled over the transom of our very tippy, hard dinghy and the freeboard went down to about four inches. We paddled back to the boat and again I needed help climbing aboard with the unaccustomed weight I was carrying.

When I was at last safe I began to feel cold. My sprained arm began to ache, and I could feel the bruises on my legs. I suppose I went into shock then because all I could do was stand there and shake. Everyone else finished bailing and putting things in relative order so we could walk around. We upped anchor and headed to Morro Bay.

I'm aware that someone else's horror story may not be enough to encourage one to wear a life jacket and/or clip onto a safety line, but I have learned. Please learn from my experience, not your own. I will always clip in after dark and in heavy weather. I probably won't wear a life jacket because I find them cumbersome and uncomfortable, but I do wear an inflatable safety harness. You'll not find me in that water again watching my boat slowly move away. Once is enough!

Janet Erken 1946-2013

28

Touching Bottom

by Geraldine Briony Hunt

Hi there, fellow sailor. You're familiar with the three stages of strategic planning for a yachting manoeuvre, aren't you? Thinking about it, talking about it, and wishing you had already done it. But have you considered the stage that comes before any of those; worrying about it?

My husband doesn't worry, or at least he doesn't verbalise it. But someone has to do the worrying, so the less concern he displays, the more I am compelled.

We own a Leopard 46 catamaran. I used to be a veterinary professor. I calmly faced lunging dogs, panicking horses, bleeding arteries. I skied the double black runs of Colorado and rafted down raging rivers. But the only thing that has ever reduced me to a trembling heap was my retirement to the peaceful life of ocean cruising.

As a long-time sailor, my main worry was the prospect of reefing the main in heavy weather, but during my inaugural blue water year I realized the thing that scared me most was the prospect of running into a reef.

When my veterinary students expressed fear I used to ask, 'Are you afraid of the idea, or are you afraid of the result?' They were usually scared that something bad might happen and they would not know how to deal with it.

I tried counseling myself in this way. 'What's the worst that can happen? The boat sinks and we drown.'

I knew that was highly unlikely, with respect to people who have lost their boats or even their lives. More likely was a tongue-biting crunch and a chunk broken from our keel. All recoverable and repairable. But rationalizing it did not help, because my fear was not rational. I had been around boats since I was a child. I worked bow on a racing yacht in Sydney Harbour. I was not scared of sailing. I was an ocean swimmer and, while I respected the ocean, I was not scared of it. So being pathologically scared of running aground came as a shock. It didn't help that I knew how to launch our new and carefully equipped liferaft, or that we had 'sacrificial keels' that could be unbolted and replaced. It wasn't the expense or inconvenience of having to haul-out for repairs, although this would be a monstrous pain in the behind. No, it was definitely 'fear of the idea' rather than 'fear of the consequences' that was bringing me undone.

Shortly afterwards, we motored through a lagoon eighty miles north of the Whitsundays. George and David – a great friend of ours – had done this countless times; picking their way through remote reefs in search of sandy anchorages with pristine water and abundant coral trout. On this afternoon, a suitable passage did not appear and the light slowly deteriorated. I felt growing panic. I could not let the others know I was shaking-scared, so I retreated to the cockpit and occupied myself unravelling about a mile of hopelessly tangled fishing line. Head down, heart racing, palms sweating, fingers working mindlessly, all the while waiting for that ghastly crunch, the shudder and then – well, I could not think beyond that.

Eventually we dropped anchor in fifty feet of dark water in the lee of the reef. It was my lowest point. I had been so scared of running aground that I could not even bring myself to sit at the helm of my own yacht, with my own husband, as we embarked on an adventure we had planned jointly for years. My wish, as I fanatically untangled the fishing line, was that we stop reef-hopping altogether. But reef-hopping was our dream. *So how was I to deal with this crippling anxiety?*

Someone once told me that when we run, we either run away from something, or we run towards it. By burying myself in fishing line, I had run away.

'I am not a runner', I told myself.

But if I could not allow myself to run away, how could I bring myself to run towards?

A leadership course once taught me that courage was the quality I admired above all others. Admitting to being scared, well that was a failure. *But was I most interested in achieving the end-goal, or protecting my feelings? Would I respect myself more by finding a way to deal with my anxiety, or by trying to appear more courageous than I was?* In explaining this to myself, I also found my answer. I wanted the end-goal, and I would do what I must to achieve it.

The first step was also the hardest. George and I shared this dream; we purchased the boat together, and I was there for every stage of the refit. We celebrated the high points of our first proper sail, our first dive off the back of the boat, catching our first fish. But sharing a dream is not just about the good stuff, it's also about the bad. So, my first and perhaps toughest challenge was admitting to George that I was scared. Not only was it a test for me, it was a test for him. That night we took a cup of tea to the bow and sat under the stars.

I said, 'We have a problem. I am having a lot of anxiety about running aground.'

Thankfully, there was no quick, 'Don't be ridiculous,' or airy 'Oh, that's not going to happen.'

'Really bad anxiety,' I went on. 'I couldn't even bring myself to watch today. I sat for two hours untangling fishing line.'

George sighed. Perhaps he feared I was about to pull the pin on this cruising caper.

'I am telling you this,' I explained, 'because I need your help to deal with it.'

He sounded relieved. 'Yes. Either we do this together or we don't do it at all.'

This was validation that we did, indeed, share the same goal. Someone else can't magically give you their courage, but knowing they have your back can help you find your own.

I said, 'I think I need to sit at the helm when we're reef hopping, regardless of how anxious I am feeling.'

If we went aground I would watch it happen, not hide down below while George and someone else pursued 'our' dream. This is so critical for cruising couples. It has to be 'our' dream. We have to share the good and the bad. So, I help George as he replaces the engine seals and unblocks toilet pipes, and he helps me when I need him.

In the pristine water of the Great Barrier Reef I found it hard to judge depth. In addition to being petrified of running into a specific something, I was perpetually nervous about running into everything.

'Can you teach me about reading the reef?' I asked. 'The colours, and currents. We can practice in deeper water. I can stand at the bow and look, and you can tell me what the sounder says.'

'We'll take the dinghy over the coral bommies,' George added, 'then we can dive on them to check their depth.'

Familiarity and growing knowledge eventually boosted my confidence, and while I could never relax while we were reef-hopping, at least I did not dread it quite so much. The mere idea of running aground caused me so much distress that, when it finally happened, in a muddy harbor in Vanuatu, it came almost as a relief. We did all the things you are not supposed to do; motoring into the sun, not checking the chart properly. I was at the bow and we had just realized we were in far less water than expected when there was a huge crunch and the boat lurched. I clung to the forestay while momentum dipped the bows into the water. George turned the boat and the other side hit. The mast vibrated like a tuning fork and I wondered if it were about to come down. Then we were free; reversing, shocked, back into deep water.

Having decided that we were not about to be dismasted, I raced back to check the bilge pumps. 'Surely we were holed?' No.

We dove on the keels and found fist-sized chunks missing from each side, the defects bristling with torn fiberglass and shards of coral. Ugly, but we were able to sail back to Noumea, during which time an oil seal began to leak, giving us another reason to haul out. A week later, the damage was fixed. We discovered that our second-hand boat was no stranger to the Coral Club, as the keels had been repaired before. The unthinkable had happened and the world had not come to an end.

One year on, George and I are still reef-hopping. We both have a healthy concern about touching bottom. When I feel the old anxiety creeping up I tell myself to pursue our dream rather than shying from it. Running towards suits me far better than running away.

Bio: I am 58 years old. Long-time monohull sailors, my husband and I made a lifestyle choice to buy a catamaran. We now own a Leopard 46 and have lived aboard and cruised on her since mid-2016. We have taken her up the Queensland coast, through the outer Great Barrier Reef, to Lord Howe Island, Sydney, New Caledonia, Vanuatu, Tonga, and Fiji.

We summered over last year in the Bay of Islands, New Zealand. George (my husband) is a retired engineer and I am a retired veterinary surgeon. Between us, we seem to be able to sort out most structural, mechanical and plumbing issues, both for the boat and for ourselves. We're still working on the electrical side of things.

Our greatest loves are passage-making when the wind is good, diving off the back of the boat first thing in the morning, and catching fish in whatever way presents itself. Oh, and I love whales. I just love them. Every passage is just one long whale-watching cruise as far as I'm concerned.

www.svalchemyi.blogspot.com.au

29

The Fear of Perception

by Cally Duncan

In the sailing world there are many things to be afraid of once you are out on the water, such as storms, pirates, or breakdowns. However, you may never have the chance to realise and overcome these fears if you never make it out on the water at all. That is why I wanted to share my story of the biggest fear that I faced in my sailing journey, that could have prevented me from going sailing at all: the fear of perception.

No matter the length or extremity of your cruising plans, each person will face various judgements from the people closest to them, especially if those people are not currently part of the sailing world. These judgements are often a concern for safety but may also stretch as far and wide as concerns for social or economic well-being as well.

When deciding to become a cruiser you may often hear questions or comments such as:

'Do you even know how to sail?'
'People get killed doing things like that!'
'You have a perfectly good job, why would you give that up?'
'Do you have the money to keep up a boat?'
'Do you really want to cut yourself off from the world for days or weeks at a time?
'Won't you be lonely?'

The most important thing when you announce your plans to your family and friends is to try and anticipate how they might feel and to have a plan as to how you will approach it. Not only was this the biggest struggle for me before we bought our boat (due to my family's limited exposure to sailing), but I also think that we, as women, tend to be more concerned with how others will perceive our decisions.

Below is the approach that allowed me to get through this trying time and address my personal fear of upsetting family and friends or 'rocking the boat' as they say. I hope it can help others to get over their fears and take their own sailing adventure.

Know Your 'Why' and Know Yourself

First and foremost, you must be certain of why you want to sail. If you are unsure, the doubts of your family and friends may be a deterrent. Ponder what you will get out of it. For me, as an extrovert and traveller, sailing allows me to meet new people and see incredible destinations. For those who are introverts, you may glean more from the intellectual side of the sport or from the downtime you will have to pursue personal hobbies like writing, knitting, or photography. If you are unsure why you are doing it, your family and friends will be sceptical as well. Alternatively, if you are passionate about why you want to go, then they may catch your enthusiasm as well.

Knowing yourself, means first thinking about your personal doubts about the journey and addressing those before announcing to family and friends. For me, my major doubt was the safety aspect of sailing. First, I armed myself with literature about sailing and weather and storm tactics. Then, I found some resources on repairs and maintenance on boats. While I have not memorised every page and could not service and maintain our boat alone, I feel that I have armed myself with a foundation of knowledge and feel comfortable that with the resources on board I could research basic repairs to get back to shore safely. In a worst-case scenario, I know how to use our EPIRB and deploy the liferaft.

Once you feel confident in yourself that your doubts have been settled, you can begin to address the doubts of others and start telling friends and family.

Plan the Questions

I planned how I would respond to each person individually before I broke the news about our decision to buy a boat. I thought about what their concerns would be and tried to anticipate the hard questions that they might ask.

I knew that my parents biggest worry would be my personal safety and the concern over throwing away a career and seven years of post-secondary education. For others with aging parents, the concerns might align more closely with who will take them to their medical appointments or wondering who would help them to mow their lawn while you are away.

It is also important to remember that whatever your family's questions are, it is likely they mean well. I had to remind myself when my relatives questioned my clumsy nature, that they were actually concerned for my safety. This prevented me from reacting and feeling personally insulted by any questions they had and allow me instead to address their fears.

Plan Your Responses

Once you have anticipated their questions, it is best to plan your responses. In the heat of the moment, you may forget what you read about forecasting weather and/or heaving-to when conditions turn for the worse. Therefore, by practicing your responses, you are more likely to be ready when your family and friends ask and to address their underlying concern.

I knew that my family would not feel any better about my decision to go sailing if I reacted and told them something along the lines of, 'Well, I will just have to practice being less clumsy.' Instead, I told them about various procedures that we would have onboard our boat. I reassured them that in rough seas we would be wearing lifejackets and lifelines and explained that throughout the boat we would have handrails and handholds to hold onto while manoeuvring.

When they were concerned about my economic security, I explained our budget to them. I also outlined ways that we could make money while we were sailing. Whether it was my partner teaching scuba diving or finding maintenance work at the various marinas we would arrive in or explaining the various ways that I could find work online over the course of our journey, it was important to show them that we had a back-up plan. I also made sure to address their views on my career path by explaining that many employers would view the trip and life experience as favourable in a perspective employee as there is budgeting, team work, learning new information, planning, and many more skills exercised while onboard a boat.

Again, in the case of aging parents, perhaps already having a plan as to which relative they can call for help who lives nearby, or a yard maintenance service they can use and afford, would best alleviate their fears regarding your absence.

Know When to Move On

Being realistic about this process is also important. I knew that no matter how much I could explain or answer each question some people would continue to have doubts. That meant that part of my journey in telling my family and friends about our trip, was to accept that they would always continue to have doubts. While my parents have accepted that the trip is happening and that we cannot be deterred from sailing, they have not fully stifled their worry. They have made it clear they are not interested in visiting us on our travels and I managed to see this as a positive outcome. I had anticipated it as the best-case scenario.

Therefore, it is an important step to consider and accept what you will not be able to achieve, no matter how hard you try. Acceptance and acknowledgement of the limitations of your loved ones will buy you peace of mind that you gave it your best effort at the very least.

Enjoy Sailing

When we told our friends and family our plans we received every form of reaction: wild enthusiasm, doubt turned to mild excitement, doubt eased to acceptance and, of course, the unreassurable worry. However, once everyone knew and we did our best to help them accept and understand, we were ready to move on and make our adventure about us again.

The most important thing is to stop your fear of what others may think to prevent you from sailing.

Now, many months after telling family and friends about our plans, we are in the final stages of planning our journey. We have mere weeks to go that will entail finishing maintenance and provisioning for our initial departure. While no outcome will ever be perfect, we have the excited support of many family and friends and cannot wait to start our journey.

We wish you fair winds on your journey as well.

Bio: Cally grew up inland in Canada and never knew there was an entire community out on the water travelling the world. After a sailing trip abroad inspired her, years later she found the perfect partner to buy a boat with. Only three weeks of dating and they found their ideal boat, so they bought it with the plan to sail it from the US back to Australia. With minimal sailing experience, they set out on their journey and they share their adventures and lessons learned on their blog at https://hownottosailaboat.com

30

Surrendering to the Unknown

by Brita Marie Siepker

"Every vessel shall at all times maintain a proper look-out by sight and hearing as well as by all available means appropriate in the prevailing circumstances..." Rule 5, International Regulations for Preventing Collisions at Sea, 33 USC 1602(c).

Standing watch on a sailboat crossing the oceans means precisely that: watching. Maybe we shorten canvas as the sun is setting to be better prepared for overnight squalls; maybe we trim a bit if the wind backs or the current pushes us off our point of sail; but mostly we look out over empty seas.

Watching monotonous seas for several hours will tire your eyes and craze your mind. You are constantly looking for something – another boat approaching us, an obstruction floating toward us, a gust of wind rippling the water, a squall line darkening the sky – when in fact there is nothing to see. It's exhausting and maddening to exert so much effort to a task that will (hopefully) result in the absence of anything.

Staring into fog in the Long Island Sound, my eyes were so bleary, and my mind was so nervous that I was certain I spotted the shadows of several fishing boats that didn't appear on radar and never materialized as we approached. On overnight watches across the Pacific, where we may go weeks without seeing another boat, I mistake cresting waves lit by the moon for the sail of a (non-existent) boat. You see nothing for long enough until your eyes and mind fabricate something.

You learn to give your eyes and mind brief periodic breaks on long watches. How long and how periodic the break may be dependent upon the captain and crew. On the boats I've passaged on, we have someone awake in the cockpit at all times, though they may entertain themselves with a movie or a book or a podcast, and they may go down into the cabin to make tea or use the head. Single-handed sailors unabashedly admit to sleeping underway, some for long stretches through the night. That's right, I said it, there are boats out there without proper look-outs.

Even with a proper look-out by all appropriate means – your eyes constantly trained on the water in front of you and the horizon around you, your ears straining to hear an engine approaching, AIS and sonar up and running – many of the hazards would escape your attention. You probably won't see a waterlogged tree trunk on the lee side; you're never going to see a whale surfacing under your hull; and there's not even a hint of a submerged shipping container to catch your eye.

No matter how vigilant you are, from the helm at night, you won't see most obstructions, and even if you could see them, it's doubtful you could alter course fast enough to avoid hitting them. The frightening truth is there is always a chance of collision at sea with something you've never even seen.

It takes some getting used to – some internal pep talking – to surrender to the risk of the unknown. You do some rationalizations calculating the likelihood of actually making contact with something in the wide-open ocean, considering the possibility of actually contracting structural damage to the boat if you did make contact (we're moving awfully slowly, the object is not moving much faster, fiberglass is pretty tough…) and finally, relying on the fact that you're not sailing just any boat – you're sailing a tank. It's going to take more than a passing kiss in the night with flotsam to part our keel or separate the rudder. *We're good. I've got this.*

(If anyone is replaying scenes from All Is Lost in their minds right now, please rewind and notice that when Robert Redford's boat hits the shipping container, the sea is becalmed; I think that there is no way a container could be moving fast enough to make that sized hole in those conditions.)

After I've done my rationalization, I remind myself that as long as we aren't plowed into by a large commercial vessel, we're going to survive. We may take on water; the boat may sink if the hole is big enough or if the pumps give out; we may lose all of our worldly possessions; but the liferaft will keep us afloat long enough for a rescue to arrive; and our navigation and communication equipment (redundant to the umpteenth level) will alert the rescuers where to come. I generally try to avoid participating in activities where I may die (it's a good rule of thumb, I think), so we're good on that front.

(If anyone is rereading passages from Moby Dick and In The Heart Of The Sea in their minds right now... Yes, whales are a concern. We try not to enrage sea animals that can sink our boat. And it's 2018, not 1820; we have EPIRBs and VHF and SSB radios and GPS and waterproof watches and sextants. We will not float for ninety-five days at sea waiting for a rescue).

To avoid colliding with another vessel, we report our location on AIS, and follow nearby vessels' locations on AIS; we use our navigational lights and scan the horizon for other vessels' nav lights; and in limited visibility we use radar to identify any obstructions in our path. If we do see anything, we steer a wide berth, especially when the vessel is much larger than us or is moving much faster than us or is another sailboat. Being vigilant and conservative significantly reduces the likelihood of collision with another vessel, which lets me sleep soundly at night while I'm not on watch.

I don't mean to sound cavalier about my safety or the safety of other vessels in my path. I take my watches very seriously. If I'm too tired to keep my eyes open, I ask for relief. If I'm unsure of an approaching vessel or shore, I ask for a second opinion. If the weather conditions are more than I'm comfortable with, I ask for help to furl the sails or heave-to. I have read the books and the blogs – the stories of collisions, of ships sunk at sea, of captain and crew drowning – and they stay with me and keep my heart pounding and my eyes peeled through every watch. The true story of Ten Degrees Of Reckoning stays with me the most. It's a story of cruisers like me, on a monohull sailboat approaching the shore of New Zealand; they were hit by a commercial vessel in the middle of the night; the mother survived to watch her husband and two children drown, to see the ship motor away and never face justice. It is a tragic story that breaks your heart and makes you re-evaluate your decision to surrender to the risks.

But just like I couldn't let the tales of traffic accidents in New York keep me from biking the city streets, and no one lets the stories of fatal car accidents keep them from driving a car, I can't let the stories of shipwrecks keep me from sailing the seas. Eventually the fear of the unknown subsides, and the trust in your sturdy vessel and your vigilant watches prevails. Be safe, sailors.

Bio: Brita Siepker learned to sail at the Manhattan Yacht Club in New York. She has been cruising full time since January 2015 and is currently circumnavigating with the World Arc 2018/2019. You can follow her adventures at: www.lifeiswater.com.

31

Am I a Real Blue Water Sailor?

by Ursula Münchinger

On the second night of our crossing Biscay Bay I lay in bed, it is pitch black, the boat is shaking wildly in the waves and when the waves smash it sounds as if we've hit a rock.

I close my eyes and wish I could be on land, safe and sound. Anywhere, but not here. I ask myself, *Am I really a blue water sailor?* And the honest answer: I'm probably not. But what has happened so far? Wasn't it my dream for the last few years to leave my boring, mundane life in Germany? That's what I wanted; to go sailing with my partner, be on the sea, explore new countries, and see the world. I have been sailing before. Okay, I used to sail on bigger boats and in the Mediterranean Sea during summer. Here in the Biscay things are different.

After three-and-a-half days crossing the Biscay Bay we arrived safely in Spain, but I felt shattered. I had to be honest to myself, I don't like night-shifts, I hate the waves and the feeling of being alone on the sea. Being lost. Well, maybe we just had a bad start. And what about us? Our whole relationship is based on the dream of going sailing and exploring the world like this. What will happen if I tell Alex that I doubt myself? I decided to keep going and not tell anyone about my fears and doubts. I hoped it would pass and the problem would solve itself. Well, two years later I can tell you: it didn't. Problems and fears don't disappear by themselves.

I recognized that as soon as the boat starts heeling, and we have more wind than forecast, I freeze, and Alex complains, justifiably. I started thinking, if we could have a bigger boat than a ten-meter steel boat, with a center cockpit, and a higher freeboard, that would help. We changed boats. Now I have all of this, but I am still scared. In the end, it is not the boat, it is me. It is one thing when someone tells you this, but quite another when you reach that point yourself. Neither the one thing nor the other is comfortable. Somewhere along the way I lost trust in myself; the trust and belief that I could handle any situation by myself. On the one hand it's a depressing thought, on the other hand – a good one. Who should be able to change that, if not me?

So, I have to work on myself. That must be possible. We met an American guy who is 62 years old. He has sailed in his boat that is nothing more than a 25-foot nutshell, across the Atlantic. Alone. With a freeboard that is slightly higher than our dinghy. He seemed to have a good trip. But that challenged me. How can it be that he managed to sail America to Europe in a tiny boat and I can't handle the short trip from Portugal to Madeira in our 44-foot Moody? There must be a solution.

First, I searched the Internet about fear itself. This type of senseless fear, not the good one that makes sense. You can be scared about not having enough money at the end of the month to pay your bills. This is a realistic fear, when you have more expenditures than income. You can make a plan, focus on what is important and only spend money on those items. At the end of the month you'll receive your paycheck and the worry disappears.

With some types of fear, it doesn't end, and it doesn't have to be realistic at all. Even though your rational brain knows that there is nothing you should worry about, there is the fear. Just in case that imagined Armageddon is about to become real. This fear can cause physical symptoms such as a higher pulse, shallow breathing, an uneasy stomach and clammy skin. People with this kind of fear have a high imagination. Unfortunately, this imagination can lead to dark places. As if a little witch is sitting inside your head never shutting up and only focusing on the bad things.

I learn that, in our brain, we have something called the amygdala and the frontal cortex. Usually, both work together fine. The eye sees something curled up laying in the shadows and the amygdala screams: *A snake!* The frontal cortex, pure rationality, says: 'Let's go, have a look. Oh, it's only a rope, nothing to be scared about.' The amygdala is happy now and drinks its coffee.

What kind of human would amygdala be like with its characteristics? It would be the annoying neighbor who only complains about a bad life, the little child that runs around while holding his ears and screaming, 'I can't hear you! I can't hear you.' It can't sit still and as soon as things don't go the way it was planned it becomes completely out of hand. The frontal cortex is pure logic, but it just can't argue against that fear mongering.

Okay, I learnt that I have a little thing in my head that has a right to be there but has to be kept in bounds. *Am I mad now?* No, after a completely non-representative survey among my sailing friends, I recognize that women are usually the ones who admit they scare more easily; there are others who feel like me. Great, maybe I'm nuts, but I am not alone, and I can work on it.

Well, trust is something that is lost easily, but not as easily gained back. So, we sail out in good conditions and then slowly increase the level of difficulty. It becomes a bit like the waves are not my friends, they are more like undesired relatives at Christmas, that I can have an armistice with.

The amygdala hits not only when waves hit the boat, but also when Alex and I have an argument. It sometimes seems difficult to find the right words that I understand. When I think I say something completely logical, Alex looks at me as if I need to see the doctor soon. He thinks I am making fun of him and my reaction towards his disbelieve and aggression is anger. We have a fight about nothing more than the colour of the cockpit; we create a display of angry words that we could sell tickets for.

Maybe somebody knows what I'm talking about? As soon as we fight, Alex withdraws himself and that can take days. If I want to talk, I get either no answer or I hear a grumbling noise. While he climbs on the next mental tree, things in my head turn wild. *Does he still love me? Is it over now? Where shall I go then? What shall I tell my parents?* His silence provokes my imagination to think of divorce, but it is all in my head. But, after a while he climbs down from the tree and starts talking again. That's the point when I need to kick my own ass and force myself to talk to him. To be able to shut up that little babbling witch in my head. Not easy, especially for me, as I am the 'avoider'. I avoid discussions that are unpleasant, and I don't ask questions where I might receive answers I don't like.

To overcome my own shadows of fear and talk to my partner it took three years and a bunch of nerves. Sure, other women may find it easier to talk about topics they don't like, but I have always fled such situations.

For all of you who are like me: Just do it. Yeah, I know, sounds easier than it is. We got a bigger boat and it helped, but I still get scared when it gets dark and I can't see what's coming. Only going out when the skies are clear and the moon is shining helps. I still sit in the cockpit feeling the fear crawling up my spine as soon as it is dark, and I recognize that the situation is fine, that I can handle it, it makes me feel better. And I am not alone. Alex knows about my weakness and helps as much as he can, after I found the courage to tell him. My wish is to keep going and follow my dream, this wish is bigger than the fear of failure. I always ask myself: *What is the worst that can happen? Drowning, losing the boat?* So, I create an 'evacuation plan' in my head. If we really need to abandon the boat, we still have our security net of a rescue vest, liferaft and EPIRB. And the belief that I can endure everything as long as he is close and we are together. When he comes down to my bunk, he lays his arms around me and I start to ease and let go. I know I can be bigger than I think I am. And you can, too.

Bio: My name is Ursula, I am 34 years old and I have lived together with my partner on a sailboat for the last two years. At the time of writing this story we are in Portugal, enjoying the summer. I am actually a farmer and came, by chance, to sailing (but that's another story) where I met my future husband and sailing partner. We bought a boat together, sold everything we had, rented out our flats and went sailing. So far, we found the most lovely places and people along the way.

https://my-life-in-flip-flops.com/

32

Life Untethered

by Anna Ash

It was the night before my first ocean passage. Skipper Gary and I were leaving Australia, crossing the Coral Sea and heading for New Caledonia. We were both nervous and a small worm of fear had burrowed its way into my mind, feeding on my insecurities. Yet although I feared my first offshore passage, I was more afraid of not doing it.

We are a good team. We had transformed *Ballyartella*, a half-completed ketch, into *Zefr*, our blue water cruiser, and then sailed the East Australian coast to get to know the boat and each other. It was a shake-down cruise for ship and relationship, and we survived. The challenges we had faced, like anchoring off the Great Barrier Reef with no land in sight, had brought out our individual strengths: courage and caution. My default position was often one of fear, whereas Gary was mostly cool as a sea cucumber. Gary is the kind of man who tackles fears head on. He was afraid of heights, so he became an arborist, wielding a chainsaw at great heights and lopping tree limbs. I had more sailing and navigation experience, but after a few rough trips (*who goes out in a strong wind warning?*) I was now easily unnerved.

Sleep evaded me. In the chill and darkness before dawn, I was thinking that I'd pull-out and fly to meet him in Noumea. Out of that darkness, the strong women in my life crowded around and buoyed me up. My mother, Vera, who survived the bombing of her home in England in the Second World War; my friend, Kristi, who set new sailing records with the Sailors with disABILITIES crew; my Koori women friends who single-handedly care for several generations of family members. Dad dropped in too, 'If I can captain a landing craft of men to D-Day and help liberate France, you, my daughter, can manage a short jump across the Coral Sea!'

They were right. How could I back out now? How could I wave goodbye from the dock, return to a safe but empty lounge room, and then a few days later board a crowded flight to meet Gary in Noumea? I recalled the sense of achievement after we returned from Bligh Reef where we snorkelled amongst pristine coral and prolific fish life. That was a great feeling and I wanted more of it. I quickly rolled out of bed, red-eyed but determined to cast out that worm of fear. We were well prepared and had used a weather forecaster to confirm our departure date, I couldn't turn back now.

Customs arrived and after half-an-hour of form-filling and a niggling anxiety, we were cleared to leave Australian waters. We pulled in our lines and stowed the fenders for the foreseeable future. With our red ensign flying at the stern we hoisted full sail and headed out of Moreton Bay. I could only just see Cape Moreton as the sun set astern and we feasted on steaming bowls of fettucine carbonara and waved Australia goodbye. I was so used to sailing north and south along the coast, that sailing east just seemed wrong. Not wrong, just different, I corrected myself. In a good way, I added.

I slept for a while then got up for the nine-to-midnight watch. *Zefr* gently dipped and rose over a long rolling swell. The moon slipped above the horizon, lighting up a silver path for us to follow. So many stars. So few people. No mobile reception. We were a small self-sufficient ship, untethered, catching the ancient trade winds across the vastness of this blue globe.

Day two passed uneventfully, which is a good thing when at sea. At first glance there seemed to be nothing out there. Certainly, there were no ships or islands, just a couple of sea mounds to avoid in case the seas above them were disturbed. Yet as I relaxed into the journey, the ocean was entertainment enough. The sun arced westwards, a couple of dolphins hitched a ride, and a tired booby tried to land on the bow rail. The brisk northerly wind dropped for a couple of hours and then shifted to the south east. We pulled the headsail across to the other side and just kept sailing. Every day was another 160 nautical miles closer to a sheltered anchorage.

Sailing can be characterised as long periods of peace followed by brief moments of far too much excitement. It was day three, the winds and the seas were up, and we were testing the new rigging, rollicking along at eight knots. It was time to drop the mainsail to reduce speed. Gary went to the mast, I turned *Zefr* into the wind and we faced the lumpy swell and breaking waves. I was afraid that we would cop a wave over the decks and Gary would be washed over the side. My knees were shaking, and I was sweating with fear, and I wasn't the one leaving the cockpit! I pulled myself together, *You've got one job to do. Just keep her bow to the wind so the sail can be dropped.*

Gary released the main halyard, and as the sail came down, so too did the boom, and it swung out over the side of the boat. The quick release clip on the topping lift had come loose. The sail caught some wind and pulled the traveller car with great force to one end and blew the end cap off the track. Gary pulled down the bulk of the sail, and I grabbed a hand full of mainsheet and brought the boom back on board and secured it. The topping lift was swinging free – we couldn't catch it in these seas – so we pulled it to the top of the mast. We found a replacement end for the traveller and screwed it in. *Zefr* was now bowling along under jib and jigger at a more comfortable six knots. My heart rate settled back to normal. Gary looked at me, there was relief in his eyes. We'd worked well together in a challenging situation and I started to believe that we could do this.

Days four and five saw some rough seas and Gary was exhausted. I took a longer night watch so he could catch up on sleep, my confidence was growing and sailing at night no longer frightened me. Gary helped in the galley, he fried the steak, I mashed potato, and together we sat down for a hearty meal while *Zefr* bowled along in the steady trade winds. We were working better together under pressure and no longer yelled or blamed each other for mishaps. Our relationship was not just surviving this ocean crossing, it was strengthening.

We approached the reef of New Caledonia early in the morning of day six and hove-to until there was enough light to enter Passe de Dumbèa, with the big ocean swell crashing on the reef on both sides. Amèdèe Lighthouse welcomed us to the smooth waters of lagoon sailing. The sun rose above the mountains of the big island as we hoisted the French and quarantine flags and motored into Port Moselle Marina. This was the first time that we had travelled under our own steam to another country, and we couldn't wait to step ashore! French cruising friends caught our lines and thrust a bag of warm croissants into my hands.

Glorious weeks were spent cruising New Caledonia's southern lagoon, exploring unspoilt reefs and enjoying freshly caught coral trout washed down with crisp vin blanc. We shared sundowners, meals and stories with cruisers from all over the world. We also shared a sense of achievement of having sailed across oceans to arrive in this idyllic cruising ground.

During the six-day ocean passage I was at times uncomfortable and anxious, however I had faced my fears, gained confidence in ship and relationship, and now I was free to enjoy this cruisers' haven.

Bio: Having conquered her fear of ocean passages, Anna, with skipper Gary, has recently sailed their ketch *Zefr* through Indonesia, Malaysia, and Thailand. Freed from the shackles of work, they plan for more cruising of Asia and the Pacific in between boat jobs. They are loving the life afloat.

Sailing with *Zefr* YouTube channel:
https://www.youtube.com/channel/UCnu6eh8vGanaPi3zQGPrhLw

33

Capsizes and Camping

by Alenka Caserman

I'm still not sure what made me decide to buy myself a sailboat and learn how to sail, but I'm very glad I took the first step. I had no clue about sailboats and I have never sailed before. Absolutely clueless about anything boat related, I found a dirt cheap, second-hand Hobie 14 and I bought it without knowing what I was getting myself into. I figured that whatever goes wrong at least the damage won't be high. I asked my co-worker whether I should take some sailing lessons, but he assured me that I should be able to figure it out on my own after reading up on some sailing theory and having a good old crack at it. Being a little too impatient to do extensive reading I found some educational material on points of sail on YouTube. The theory seemed very basic and I was confident that I'd be able to work it out. I was very keen to test the new purchase in practice.

Next challenge was how to "assemble" the vessel. YouTube came to my assistance once again. I also took snaps of various boat bits and sent them to my co-worker via text messages to obtain instructions about what to do with them. I'm amazed that my little boat even managed to stay rigged during my first expedition as I later found out that various bits weren't attached where they were supposed to be. After a practice "assembly" run it was time to find a real launching spot.

Not knowing a single thing about winds or tides in the bay I picked a boat ramp fairly close to home. My dear husband volunteered to assist with the rigging, to witness my first attempt and duly take some photographic evidence. We carefully assembled the beach cat and lowered it into the water. I hopped on and engaged my "101 sailing theory".

Initially things were not going great and the boat drifted towards a jetty. There were several amused spectators. After about five minutes of turning the rudders this and that way and figuring out how the pulley blocks for the main sail work I slowly started moving away from the jetty. I was instantly delighted to be solely responsible for making the wind powered craft go somewhere. About an hour later things were going splendidly and I figured how to make the floating marvel of two pontoons zip through the water at an exciting speed. I was so mesmerised by the joy of sailing that I didn't even think of which way I was going or how that would affect my ability to return. I'm not really sure I knew how to stop the boat and I didn't imagine that much else could possibly go wrong.

Then I was suddenly upside down about 10 kilometres north of where I started with no idea how to get myself out of that pickle. The twitchy beast gave me very little indication that it was about to slingshot me forward and topple over on me. It seems like it all happened in an instant, joy quickly turned to panic and a big, 'oh no'. I'm glad that I was at least sensible enough to wear a life jacket. As the catamaran flipped forward it turtled straight away. I had no righting rope and no knowledge of how to approach it. The best I managed to do is flip the boat on its side from where it would repeatedly sink back into the fully inverted position.

Long story short: after some time two jet skiers found me helplessly perched atop of my inverted boat drifting between two islands and the coastguard was summoned to tow my sorry ass back to shore. The coastguard righted the cat with a long rope and a powerboat. It was a sad sight as the rudders were broken, the sail was badly mangled and the sidestays so loosely attached that the mast looked like it was close to falling down. The rescuers instructed me to hop back on the little boat as it was towed back a to marina. It was my tow of shame. I later made a sizeable donation to the fine establishment of volunteers that came to pluck me out of the water.

I would say my sailing adventures started with no fear because I had no concept of what could go wrong and then I instantly acquired a healthy dose of fear on my first attempt.

I approached my subsequent attempts with a lot more caution and sensibility as I learned that these small vessels capsize very easily and without much warning. Any misconception about romantic sunset sailing, sipping on champagne and nibbling on canapes is quickly thrown overboard on a Hobie. Capsize is, in fact, an inevitable part of the learning process and the experience more akin to bucking bull rodeo riding. Very different to what I imagined when I set out to learn how to sail but also far more fun than I could ever imagine.

I have had no more serious misadventures since. On my second attempt I did not go any further than 200 metres from shore and every slight puff of wind made me terribly nervous. It took many more sessions on the water to learn the basics, each time pushing through the fear, repeating over and over again. My biggest fear was that the boat would capsize, and I wouldn't be able to right it. Being able to recover the boat is key to being able to sail confidently. Various methods of righting were advised and tested but, in the end, no matter what I did, the rules of physics were stacked against me. Unless conditions were ideal with wind, tide, and waves all assisting, my body weight did not provide sufficient leverage to right the boat. I ended up stuck in this precarious position many more times and required assistance from another sailor or a power boat to right the boat. No amount of advice on proper technique made the process easier for me. Every time the boat capsized I became stressed knowing that there'd be a high chance that I would get tired after multiple attempts at righting and I would need to hail for help. Many times, the boat would turtle which makes matters even more challenging.

Finally, relief came in the shape of a bulbous top-of-the-mast attachment called Bob and a bag that could be filled with water to give me more righting leverage. These two little things gave me freedom and confidence and I still remember the first time I ventured a bit further out than I previously dared, mindful that I was pushing the limits of my own confidence. On a day with fine wind I ducked out past the islands into the open bay, very close to where I had my first misadventure. Having a jolly good time, I wanted to swing out on the trapeze to really get going. In the excitement, I forgot to hook in my harness and I did a spectacular backflip into the water. Still holding the main sheet, the boat dragged me after, and then it capsized. This sort of situation would normally have me sweating and feeling helpless but this time I trusted that I can get back up and get going. I swam back to the boat, climbed on the bottom hull, pulled out the stowed righting bag and prepared my righting rope. I slipped a few times when I was filling up the bag as the boat was rocking in the intense chop, but I knew I just had to keep going. The nerve-racking moment came when I leaned out and swung the righting bag behind my back. The boat slowly started to come up and popped right back on her pontoons. I felt victorious and I knew I was ready for the next chapter.

In April I had a few extra days off for a long weekend. I packed up my camping gear with a portable stove, food, water, portable solar panel, and a battery bank. I packed everything in three drybags, strapped them on the trampoline of my baby boat, and off I went to the nearby Moreton Island where I camped and sailed for five days in utter bliss.

The return journey took a slightly unexpected turn with the wind forecast changing and giving me a 40 km upwind journey in 20 knots or so. I had barely got past the challenge of being confident that I can right the boat and this new challenge came along, more mental than physical. I set out determined that I would not capsize with my camping gear strapped to the trampoline if I can avoid it. After six hours of slogging it upwind and being tossed about like a ragdoll I made it back to my starting position with zero capsizes.

I'm sure I have many more challenges ahead of me and I shall take them on one by one as they come.

Bio: A self-proclaimed geek and an IT consultant by profession, Alenka only recently discovered passion for sailing after buying a used Hobie 14. She's always liked the sea and water activities and has been scuba diving since a young age, but sailing is a new obsession for her. Now she wonders where the wind will take her.

34

What do you do with Your Fear?

by Gabriela Damaceno

This question always comes to my mind when I'm at sea, whether it's sailing, surfing or snorkelling. I have been in love with the sea since I was a child and being surrounded by the immensity that is the ocean makes me feel good. But at the same time, it makes me very afraid.

Growing up, December and January were always the most exciting months of the year for me. That scent of sunscreen and hot summer nights remind me of the incredible days I spent on the north coast of São Paulo. The salty skin and burning sensation in my eyes were the signs of a well-spent day on the beach. I was born and raised in the largest city in Latin America, surrounded by tall buildings and paved streets, a true concrete jungle. The summer holidays for me were synonymous with the beach.

São Paulo is about 100 kilometres from the coast and going to the beach was something that only happened during school holidays. I had no relatives who lived on the coast or had a summer house. My parents never owned a boat, or practised surfing or fishing. The closest to marine life that my father came was working at a fish stall. Yet, even though it was not something that was part of my life growing up, the sea always fascinated me. That immensity of water, possessing incredible force, moves me in a way that I cannot put into words.

When I was accepted into university, I moved to Florianópolis. With 42 beaches, two lagoons, sand dunes and a rich historical and cultural heritage, the city was (and still is) a paradise for a young girl from São Paulo. There I decided to join a solar boat team that competed in events around the world, and during this volunteer experience, I had my first contact with seamanship and nautical terminology. With this team, I had the opportunity to visit tall ships in the Netherlands, steer a boat driven by the energy of the sun, and kayak in the Dutch channels.

If that was not enough, I lived on an island for five years, tried to surf many times, and lived on a 25-foot long sailboat in Australia. I have to confess that I am still afraid of the sea. *But, Gabriela, what do you mean?* It is something that psychology might be able to explain – and there's even a strange name for it: Thalassophobia is the fear of the sea. I love and want to live near the ocean, but I feel afraid to surf or sail.

After finishing college in Brazil, I decided to pack up and move to Australia. Not content with the change of continent, I decided to do something different and went to live on board a sailboat. My goal is to reconcile my career in digital marketing management with life on the water. And who knows, maybe a sailing trip around the world eventually. I am so excited about this new challenge that I frequently dream that we are sailing in Tahiti, or that *Migaloo*, the famous white humpback whale, is cruising with us.

However, on my first outing on the open water, I felt terrified. So much fear built up inside me that I could not have fun. I'm so clueless about sailing and English is not my first language, so much of the nautical terminology doesn't make any sense to me. Just to give an example of how confusing it can be, the Portuguese words for 'push' and 'pull' sound like their opposites in English. So, imagine the mess during my first marina docking! I was so confused by all the terms and so afraid to make a mistake that could make our boat sink that I freaked out and didn't have fun at all. That fear was making me feel weak and guilty.

After returning to Brisbane, where the boat is moored, I began to reflect on this mix of fear and passion that I have for the sea. I came to the conclusion that I have two options: either I give up living what I have always dreamed of, or I challenge myself to overcome it. I cannot change what I feel. But I have the power to decide what to do with it. I believe that the fear of new challenges can lead you two ways: either it blocks you from living your dream, or it pushes you toward what you are looking for.

To use this feeling to my advantage, I decided to look for tools to improve my confidence in the water. Having proper physical preparation, expanding my technical vocabulary/knowledge, and practising the things that I would like to feel more comfortable doing are some examples of things that I am applying to my routine to make me feel fearless.

The other day I was reading the book Women Of Discovery: A Celebration Of Intrepid Women Who Explored The World written by Milbry Polk. The book tells fantastic stories of brave women across many continents, of visionaries, adventurers, artists, and scientists. While I was reading it, I started to imagine the number of scary situations that must have crossed the paths of these women and how they didn't let it put them down. I have no doubt that they felt fear at different points in their lives, but they didn't let it block them from moving forward.

Feeling fear when you face an unusual situation is part of human existence. But what we do with this fear is what makes the difference in life. When I see my boat (my home), tilting at 45 degrees while speeding through the water, instinctively my will is to give up and return to the marina. But if I love the sea so much, I have to get over it, to follow my heart and live the life that I want to.

Bio: Gabriela is a Brazilian journalist, currently living in a 25-foot sailboat moored in Brisbane. She's a curious, adventurous girl who enjoys visiting new places and being in touch with different cultures. She's already called Florianópolis, Buenos Aires, and now Brisbane home, having visited more than ten countries. She's passionate about the ocean and living the digital nomad lifestyle.

www.vitaminseablog.com

35

Thunder and Lightning

by Lena Kempén

I have been sailing in Croatia, Greece, the Caribbean, and the Gulf of Bothnia. My fear is the same wherever I go. There are no sharks in the Baltic Sea. There are no treacherous shallows in the Adriatic Sea, as there are in the northern waters of Sweden. So, what could then possibly be similar?

Ever since I was a child I have had to struggle with this fear inherited from my mother. I remember waking up in the middle of the night in our summer cottage noticing the flashes through the blinds. It didn't take long before Mum ordered me and Dad to dress and run out to the car, which was supposed to be the safest place during a thunderstorm. The lightning, the counting 1,001 – 1,002 – 1,003 – waiting for the thunder to hit our ears affected me tremendously. Soon I was as scared as my mother was.

I was convinced not to pass this fear on to my children.

In summer we always spent our holidays sailing around in our beautiful and peaceful archipelago. One day we anchored in a small bay and used the dinghy to get ashore. The warm and sunny weather shifted quickly. Dark clouds came floating over the treetops and soon I heard an unmistakable sound. I looked at the sole mast in the middle of the bay and decided to stay ashore.

My son and my daughter played in the sand. The noise came closer. It started to drizzle. The children ran happily in the water. Then it began pouring down.

'Mum let's go back to the boat!'

'Oh, no! Come here! Let's stand under this small tree instead!'

I figured that among all these huge trees the possibility for a hit in the lowest one would be much more unlikely, than that of a hit in the mast. (Yes, I am aware that fear makes you a bit nutty!)

My soaked children stood shivering under the tree while the lightning became more intense.

'Can we go back now?'

'No, let me tell you a fairy tale about a troll…'

There we stood, the children wrapped up in bath towels and me telling a made-up story, while the thunder passed over the island. I hoped that my brisk behaviour wouldn't reveal my tense nerves. *Did I succeed?* No! My daughter is now as scared of thunder storms as I am.

My own solution to cope with my fear is to have absolute control of the weather forecasts. I have a lot of apps in my iPhone and check them frequently. Bad weather can of course appear unexpectedly but with the help of my apps and some good luck I have managed to avoid real heavy thunder storms at sea so far. With the boat tied up, preferably close to land, and high trees and possibly with a sip of whiskey I cope with my fear.

Bio: Living in the very north of Sweden. Active in the network "Ta rodret, kvinna!" = "Women, take the helm!" Writing in Swedish boat-magazines (freelance).

36

The Wolf

by Annabel Stewart

I was terrified of sailing as a kid. Terrified. Every weekend for a big chunk of my 1980s' childhood, our parents would cheerfully bundle me and my brothers into the car and drive us down to our little Contessa 32 in Lymington, on the south coast of England.

They would then proceed to subject us to a weekend of family sailing fun; out to The Needles and back, or over to Cowes on the Isles of Wight, or even, daringly, across the English Channel to France.

They would display every sign of enjoyment during these periods of torture. From loading the marina trolley with tins of chicken in white sauce and chocolate biscuits, to huddling over the radio at midnight listening to the shipping forecast, to bouncing along over the whitecaps at a 45-degree angle with scudding clouds above: their yellow-wellied figures pretty much constantly radiated pleasure.

For them, this was the highlight of their week. They got to escape the daily grind and blow the cobwebs away on the Solent. My older brothers would treacherously collaborate in this intolerable charade. Stow the lines? Will do. Hank on the jib? No problem, Mum. Take the tiller while I take a fix with the RDF? Of course, Dad!

Memory could possibly be playing me false, but I remember spending every single minute on the boat in the grip of fear. I think I spent the entire time lurching from gloomy trepidation to severe panic and back again. I'd worry about the weather. I'd worry about losing sight of the shore. I'd worry about other boats – especially tankers – ominously heading our way. I'd worry if we heeled too much. I'd worry about mooring, about accidentally jybing, about picking up piles, about someone falling in. I felt like everyone on the boat had a job: Mum did sail changes on the foredeck, Dad was navigator, brother #1 was helmsman, brother #2 caught the mackerel off the stern. My job was to worry. Because no-one else did it. Didn't they realise what a risky occupation this sailing business was?

In my defence, you have to realise that this was an exciting (read: unpredictable) time in sailing. The new Whitbread Round-the-World Race was attracting a lot of interest, particularly for including a female skipper. Controversial stuff. The newspapers were full of the ongoing inquest into the tragically disastrous '79 Fastnet Race, plus the BOC Challenge had also been recently launched to quite a fanfare. Closer to home, my mother regularly raced a quarter-tonner in the Solent and would come home full of tales of exciting mark-roundings, broken equipment, and man-overboards. I knew that you had to be vigilant, this sailing business was no picnic.

So, I spent most weekends and the majority of school holidays in a state of fear. Entirely of my own doing, but very real nonetheless. As soon as I was old enough to have a say in our family time, I advocated vociferously to stay on dry land, preferably in the vicinity of horses, and was sad but relieved when the family boat was sold.

So, it was curious (and totally illogical) that, fast-forward fifteen years, I decided that the sea was calling me. I'd spent my 20s working my way up the corporate career ladder and was enjoying a measure of material success. But I felt that adventure was eluding me, and I needed to go to sea to find it.

Completely disregarding my paralysing fear of all things nautical, I threw myself into various sailing courses and built up my sea-time. I decided to take the gruelling Yachtmaster Offshore exam, mainly to avoid being relegated to the traditional female jobs like toilet-cleaning and spud-peeling, and was delighted to pass.

I spent the next ten years working on boats of all shapes and sizes, all over the world, conquering every single one of those fears.

I learnt how to climb a mast with my mouth full of the acid taste of terror, swallowing it down. I learnt that I could decipher a synoptic chart and pinpoint the right day to leave on passage. I learnt I could manage an all-male delivery crew. I learnt I could change an in-line fuel-filter in a seaway when the engine won't start and there's no wind and you have lots of shipping bearing down on you. At night. I learnt that I could berth a large heavy monohull in the tightest of marina berths, stern-to in the Mediterranean fashion – single handed – with most of St Tropez watching. I learnt to enjoy dolphins leaping in the bow wave. I learnt I could enjoy the quiet secret elation of a solo night watch under a full moon on a glorious beam reach. I learnt about the satisfaction of getting a boat across a vast ocean, safely, without hitting anything or anyone falling off.

I learnt all these things, and I learnt that fear could be moulded, squashed, pushed away into a secret corner of yourself so that your life, your journey, your adventure can then be allowed to unfold.

But what I didn't learn was that, much like the sea, fear comes in many guises. And, like the sea, just when you think you've got it sussed, it comes back and bites you on the bum.

I thought I had my fear of the sea and sailing conquered. So many thousands of sea miles, so many voyages and escapades. I knew sailing! I had a healthy respect for the sea, but I wasn't scared of it.

My husband and I decided, after a decade ashore, to go down to the sea again. We bought a boat, loaded the kids on board and sailed off into the sunset.

My old enemy, fear, and his wily cohort, danger, were waiting, out there on the eastern coast of Australia. Waiting for my children, and if they couldn't take my children, they wanted me. They were crouched behind the mainsail on every downwind passage, waiting to forcefully crash the boom onto unwary young skulls; they lurked under the pulpit with grey jaws, watching an unsuspecting child sitting on the bowsprit; they rejoiced in every unforecast blow that battered the boat until our teeth rattled and the crockery crashed in the lockers, waiting hungrily below the grey foamy face of the pounding waves.

Sailing with children was exhausting. There was danger everywhere I looked. I felt my experience actually worked against me; I knew too much, knew what could go wrong, knew what happened if you took your eye off the ball.

In the end, fear won. I was wrung out from months of battling the constant belief that I was putting my children in danger.

I wish it hadn't won. I wish I could be like the many parents around the world who are having happy and successful sailing adventures with their families. There's something broken in me, something damaged, that won't allow me to ever enjoy sailing with our children on board.

My husband was beyond disappointed. We talk of going again, when the kids are grown up and we're empty-nesters, when it's just him and me to consider. We know that we're big enough and ugly enough to look after ourselves.

You know that saying, the one about feeling the fear and doing it anyway? Well, I did that. Twice. I felt the fear and I did it anyway. The second time, it turned out the fear was bigger than me.

There's another saying, a German one: 'Fear makes the wolf bigger than he is.' It does. Fear does magnify the worry. But that wolf is there to start with. There is definitely a wolf, it's just that fear makes it even bigger.

But I'm so proud that we did it. We spread our wings, we took the road less travelled. The best thing is, I won't die wondering. I don't spend sleepless nights, wondering what it would be like. We're too busy to wonder anyway, we're plotting our next family adventure. There's a very good chance that by this time next year we'll be in a different country.

Who's afraid of the big bad wolf?

Bio: Annabel Stewart was born in the UK to sailing mad parents and seemed to spend a lot of her childhood slogging across the English Channel and peering into fog. As an adult, she did a variety of jobs, including working as a professional sailor for some years in the Med and Caribbean, before meeting her Australian husband and settling in Queensland.

Annabel's first book is due for release in 2018 and she's working on her second. She loves hearing from readers and can be contacted on:
annabelstewartwrites@gmail.com
www.theseastewarts.com

37

On Fear

by Jane Wilson

I think a lot about fear. No more than previously, but now differently. I used to make lists to deal with my insurmountable procrastination.

Afraid of: paperwork, wriggling through small dark spaces, starting a conversation, very clean people, very organised people, social faux pas, deadlines.

Not afraid of: blood and gore, broken bones, handling large animals, talking to 300 people from a stage, small-medium sized bits of farm machinery, walking solo in the wilds, fierce weather, public nude swimming (of late).

It would make me do the paperwork.

My ADHD DNA contributed to a rather hotchpotch career that spanned from starting as a vet, mostly being a winemaker and farmer, and then ending up here, on the brink of the Southern Ocean. 'Here' is a paradisiacal Tasmanian island where land and seascapes, and walking and wild weather are constant delights, when not truck driving to earn a living.

My childhood was in the Scottish West Highlands, immersed in achingly beautiful landscape. Always the ocean, a deep, cold unutterably massive ocean. A proper ocean.

I am, however, ocean-specific. Neither the North Sea nor Bass Strait do it for me – shallow, sandy, grey and treacherous. On this island, after a southerly blow, majestic masses of coldly pearlescent green-blue-white water surround me. In the night I hear the waves on the beach, my childhood.

Growing up I never sailed. I lived by the Atlantic, it both fascinated and terrified me. When the winter Atlantic storms hurled spume and fury, my father would gravely make us pause and think of the safety of those at sea. Curled up in bed listening to the banshees outside, I would try to imagine what it must be like to be caught out there in the screaming blackness. *What sort of bravery and skill was needed?*

I did try to sail. I asked my dad if he could find me a job on a sailing boat. Predictably, I ended up as a temporary cook, in the wake of a departing skipper and cook (absconded together in time-honoured fashion) on the National Trust volunteers' delivery out to St Kilda. The immortal instructions on departure were, 'It's mince on the way out and haggis on the way back, and don't worry about presentation as they'll bring it all up half an hour later.' No sailing, yet I discovered an ability to cook when seasick.

The interim years were taken up with the hotchpotch of career, family, small business, debt, worry, drought. There was some success or at least persistence. All was conducted in an amazing landscape, far away from the sea.

When things were bad, I would wake with not only worry, but also a profound and persistent ache of the soul.

Next came the modern cliché, marriage breakdown plus the mincing, disguising and discarding of my career by others in the wake of the split of commodity and land.

And then, somehow, I found my way here. To my Tasmanian island, isolated and beautiful, the ocean at the end of my bed, a sense of home, a soothing of soul. EVERYONE sailed, they all seemed to have boats, in a very egalitarian, do-it-yourself, life on the water, ripping yarns kind-of-way.

The craving started again. I begged crewing spots and sailed with new friends. I spent way too much time on the internet, boat-lusting.

Then I found her, *Erik*, my stout-hearted, large bottomed boat. I love the broad beaminess of her. I adore the workhorses of this world. I like the simplicity of them, the well-built can-do-ness with the ability to prance and show off in the right conditions.

I don't want to mast-furl a sail. I want to reef it down with rope. To see how it works and comprehend how I could possibly fix it with just the basics. My partner and I took her on and started to fix a few things. He tried to teach me. He was bloody draconian; proper coiling, knotting, scrubbing, tying up. The language, really, just who says athwart anyway?

His previous life at sea, (at one stage fishing solo in the Bass Strait for a living), meant doing things methodically… correctly. I needed this kind of discipline, because I'm afraid. Excited, but also afraid. Everything seems huge, flapping and awkward. I rush and fluster if something changes. I know it will pass when I have started to ingrain a habit of working, but oh, that fear. I'm older, stiffer, I have to find my fucking glasses.

I have a teenage dream and a menopausal mind and body.

He gave me the best advice, 'Just lift your fear threshold, start with the small things, it will get easier.' So, I started with solo tasks. First with moorings, repeatedly sneaking up to them, until I could master the nonchalant stroll forwards with the boat hook, instead of the flailing scurry.

Next were the hard-stationary things. Patient friends waiting to receive panicky phone calls and/or warps on jetties as I crept in, in a cold sweat. In my defence, *Erik* has the momentum and stopability of an elephant on ice.

My dearest girlfriend (Taurean) set sail with me bringing food, weather spreadsheets, and checklists. I hung my (Sagittarian) head out the cockpit and argued about weather, reefing, and forgot the food. On the end of the phone my partner bored me to sleep on my restless nights with his famous anchoring stories of the Bass Strait.

I found comfort zones. I loved the boat, loved hoisting the sails, hauling them down. I loved the adaptability of a ketch and the stability of a full keeled double-ender. I loved helming in weather. I deliberately set out to sail back from Hobart in stiffer and stiffer weather conditions, to learn to manage. Blithely promising my girlfriend soup and reefs. I rehearsed my fear and planned to tackle it, bit by bit.

I wanted to feel competent when, in reality, I was more and more short-sighted, scatter-brained, stiffer and slower. This was NOT supposed to happen. I felt the faint shape of a plan start to form. I wanted to feel I could get the boat back if left single-handed, through accident or illness.

I needed to rehearse. I wanted that feeling of my body taking action, doing things when the mind was reeling. So, I set out to do a solo circumnavigation of my island for my birthday. To see how it felt.

I picked unsettled weather. I was terrified and exhilarated, as I sped past home in 22 knots, everything up. I was mortified when I couldn't get the sails up on my own in a bad swell. I made really bad decisions. I had to up anchor and move in a severe weather change at dusk, panicking in the vanishing visibility. I then remembered I had taken a bearing and plotted an alternative, just up anchor and go, avoiding any hard and dry bits (sage advice from the draconian bearded one).

It's a big island. Two days later I came home just in front of a southerly, reefs in, foul weather gear on. I felt, oh SO proud as I calmly put her into the berth in a choppy swell.

Then, something happened to bring me up short – make me remember what the ocean is really like. I saw real fear. Dark, sucking fear. Not the late middle-aged titillation I was putting myself through.

In what I now know to be his PTSD plus a premonition of a stroke. I saw what it must have been like to work a boat single-handed in one of the most dangerous places in Australia, to be in the places I had tried to imagine as a child curled up in bed in the Highlands.

Hanging in a small cove on a desolate peninsula, waiting out a weather change with an angry man who had suddenly, alarmingly, wanted to go home. He wouldn't or couldn't explain. After the nasty atmosphere, arguing, recriminations and then eventually his illness and loss of ability, I finally fully comprehended.

So now my fears are different. I worry about maintenance and costs. Fortunately, I still have my bearded (shore-based) teacher. I have can-do girlfriends, and a far-sighted plan. I am going to mark my 60th by sailing up to Sydney (with crew), sitting my CYA offshore and sailing back.

I will accept my limitations, that I will be a 'yachtie' and not a deep ocean hero. I will scare myself just enough to feel that I can act if things turn bad, that I can competently skipper. I know I am profoundly privileged, I can wait something out, pick my weather and challenges. I don't have to be out there, my living doesn't depend on it.

The driving force for me is the very real understanding of the narrowing time frames of health and ability, my small window (perhaps) before parental infirmity.

My only fear now, in reality, is the fear of NOT doing it.

Bio: Jane Wilson lives on a small farm on Bruny Island in Tasmania. She is nurturing a life-long desire to sail by doing as much as she possibly can on *Erik*, her Atkins 32 ketch, a sistership to *Suhaili*, and a great boat for these southern waters. www.bullbay.com.au

38

What if...

by Elizabeth Tyler

During the many years my husband and I sailed together, first in the Baltic and later via the waterways of Europe to the Mediterranean, I often had to hide a panic attack, and had a nagging feeling of fear that I never talked about. It was irrational because my husband Max was about as competent as anyone could be at sea, so I did feel safe and secure with him at the helm. He was a merchant navy captain and later became a marine pilot before his early retirement. What nagged me were all the thoughts of '*What if*'...

What if he fell overboard, how on earth would I get him up again?

What if he had a heart attack while sailing, what would I do?

What if he was injured and incapacitated in any way. How would I get help?

What if he became seriously ill on board? Could I sail the boat alone to a safe harbour?

It happened. He did get seriously ill and although we were in a safe anchorage it was difficult to get help. He had been quite normal the day before but then woke up in the morning with no memory. At all. He didn't know who I was, where he was or what had happened. I tried calling PAN-PAN on the radio, nobody answered. I tried waving frantically to people on other boats nearby, they just waved back. I tried telling him we had to get ashore, but he didn't understand.

He wasn't in pain, but something was very, very wrong. I thought it might have been a mini stroke and hoped he would get better after a rest. I was in denial, didn't believe what I was seeing and hearing, just waiting for him to be normal again.

In the end I persuaded him to get down in the dinghy, so I could row him ashore. I couldn't start the outboard engine, had never ever done that. He was semi catatonic, staring into space and holding his flip-flops in his arms like a baby. I had to push him up the quayside ladder when we got ashore and it took ages to persuade him to hold on and put one foot over the other. None of my many 'what if' fears and fantasies had ever prepared me for a situation like this.

I got hold of a taxi to take us to a clinic in the nearest town. When a female doctor, who didn't speak much English, asked what the problem was, I had to explain the situation simply, so I told her my husband had gone crazy. 'My husband is crazy too!' she said with a big smile. I could laugh at that later but not then.

After examining him and asking him simple questions that he couldn't answer we were taken by ambulance over the mountains to the nearest hospital. This was repeated five times as we were transported from one hospital to another. I was irrationally more worried about how I would get back to the boat, now it was dark, than I was about the very serious situation! I suppose my brain couldn't handle the consequences of the actual crisis.

I rang the insurance company who arranged for a private hospital in Athens to send an ambulance to fetch us. Then we were driven at full speed with howling sirens and flashing, blue lights up and down the mountains and round hairpin bends until finally, after three hours we arrived in Athens. By this time Max was totally unresponsive and was taken to the ICU where he was put on a ventilator. The doctor told me to go to a hotel, as there was no reason for me to stay there.

The problem was that I had come away without money, credit card, passport nor any kind of ID. Needless to say, I had no change of clothes either. So, there I was at a hotel reception looking as if I was shipwrecked in dirty shorts and frayed shirt trying to get a room. I couldn't even begin to explain what had happened, I just needed to sleep. In the end the insurance company came to my rescue and I was given a room.

Max was diagnosed with HSE Herpes Simplex Encephalitis, a simple cold sore virus that had attacked his brain. He remained in the ICU for three weeks before we were transported home to Sweden where he was hospitalised for two months. The brain damage was very severe and by the time he was discharged he had the mental capacity of a two-year-old.

In the meantime, I faced new challenges every single day. Max had not only looked after the boat in every way but also the car, the house and our economy. Apart from painting, as a professional artist, I had only taken on the traditional woman's role of cooking and cleaning, both at home and on the boat. Suddenly I had to do everything myself and realised there was so much I had no idea about. From filling the car with the wrong fuel and trying to repair things with the wrong tools to paying bills from the wrong account. Then I was suddenly forced to be a full-time nurse without any kind of training or help whatsoever.

Max survived for 20 months without ever again knowing who I was. I was 67 years old when he died five years ago and I had to decide what to do with the rest of my life. I couldn't bear even thinking about selling the boat, it had been such a great part of my life.

I decided then to take on the challenge of sailing alone. Writing a blog about it became a kind of therapy. It was also written, and still is, in the hope it could encourage other women, who perhaps were tied up in a similar situation, to let the lines go and get underway. At that time I wrote, 'Maybe I'll crash into something, fall over board or just make a fool of myself and then it won't be any encouragement, but at least I'll give it a try.'

The first time I tried taking up the anchor and motoring out to sea alone I was trembling with fear. The first time I hoisted the sails I feared I had done everything in the wrong order and the first time I slept alone on the boat at anchor I was terrified every time I heard a strange noise. I did get used to it though and learned to deal with my fear and use the knowledge I obtained to strengthen myself for new challenges.

I'm often asked if I'm ever scared and my answer is always; 'Yes, scared stiff!' Like one night at anchor in the middle of a large bay when I was awakened by a very loud bang. My anchor had dragged and I had collided with another boat. The very naked, French boat owner came out and told me to ' **** off!' I tried to push the boat away but couldn't. Then he told me to take my anchor up, but in trying to it got tangled into his chain. The only thing to do was to get in the dinghy to pull myself alongside and try to reach the anchor. However, the pressure of the wind was too strong, and I couldn't lift it off. The naked Frenchman then jumped down into my tiny dinghy beside me to help! A big wave threw me off balance, so I had to hold on to him... In the end we untangled my anchor and I got away. I thought if I ever saw him again I would say, 'Sorry I didn't recognise you with your clothes on!'

During the past five years I have experienced several situations I had always feared before. My propeller has been fouled with plastic sacks, rope and fishing net but I have succeeded in freeing it each time. My dinghy was lost in the open sea but was returned after I called for help on the VHF. My outboard engine has failed so many times that I am now a strong oarswoman. It has also been drowned in seawater, but I retrieved it again and got it to work. Both my anchor windlass and GPS have failed but I fixed the power supply for them both. I feared ever having to dock backwards between boats in the dark and with a crosswind. I succeeded even though I had to try nine times!

I now sail and live aboard my boat five months a year in Greece, finding inspiration for my watercolours and acrylic paintings. I meet wonderful people and make new friends nearly every day. Overcoming my worst fears but still facing challenges has become a way of life for me and I hope to go on sailing for many years to come.

Bio: Elizabeth Tyler was born in 1946 in the UK but has lived most of her life in the Nordic countries. In recent years she has spent several months each summer in the Mediterranean, sailing, painting, writing books and producing educational videos about her painting techniques. Her boat is a 31 ft Hallberg Rassy Monsun from 1976 which she now sails alone. Her paintings have been exhibited in galleries and art museums in many countries around the world and she has held workshops and inspirational talks in Denmark, Sweden, Finland and Iceland. She is master member of the International Watercolour Society Global and member of the International Guild of Realism.
Blog : http://yachtswoman.blogspot.com
Website: www.elizabethtyler.com

39

To Crack a Mold

by P A Mcleod

For many years our clan of five would join with a group in the Florida Keys. We'd hunt lobster and explore, and in spite of what numb indifference I might have shown, those memories of wind and water, and blazing heat – burning solitude into that dreamy grand rally, were not to be forgotten. These would set the character of my life.

We had been long in the sun, skirting about looking for wrecks and other hidden treasure. Pulling the legal limit of lobster. Or trying to. Just one more stop. Then again. Dad and brother secured the boat just in from the bridge. They dove in for a quick surveillance while we, the three girls, stayed on deck to count and measure and be ready to head back when they returned. It's amazing how adrenaline can blind you to time.

I was ten. I was bored. Ready to be loosed from my family. I drifted away with the freshening winds and the air pressure drawing circles around me. I watched the clouds roll and mingle their darkening folds. I squeezed the landscape through my sweaty eyes and sank into that belly. And watched, in my haze as a silent fear came heavy and unsettled - like turned cream in a teacup.

My eyes opened. The anchor wasn't holding. Our little open fisherman was being pushed steadily and bobbed toward the rocks at the foot of the bridge. The current was swift. And our men had vanished.

There was a dead weight of calm on the boat. My mother's eyes empty with resignation. She turned the ignition. And again. No catch. She had never stood more than to hold the helm for my father. My brother, always custodial to the captain.

I don't recall other details like whether we had VHF or not, but it wouldn't have mattered. These weren't her tools. We tried yelling, but the wind would have none of it. We had no magic notions, only the ugly film of helplessness as the boat dragged on.

I'm sure I counted a forever of seconds before catching my brother's head pop to the surface. Masked behind his gear and hundreds of yards away, we saw his panic.

Maybe we needed a saviour. Or maybe fear inspired greatness, but my brother moved with speed I could not have imagined from him. Within a blink, he was there yelling for us to raise the anchor, engaging the motor, and pulling us away from the crags. The sky then split with a roar and released its hold.

My sister, two years older, does not recall this day. My mother sees the memory as no different than most. I hardly speak to my brother. And my father has not long been passed. But for me, this memory holds weight. It encapsulates a resolve, the meaning of which I am still trying to riddle free.

I left Florida when my time for roaming came. I had no plans to return. I was going to create a new story, new characters, new terrain. I went to the mountains and set about the change. But every good plot has it's twist and here I am, again on home waters, many grey years later. I would never own a boat though. That had been my mantra. Ha! This wicked glee only proved to wake the great game player, and I find myself caught in another corner move.

I now own my father's last boat, his world, at least when he was my hero. This is where he poured all his joy and energy and love of rules and adventure. It's where he reigned as king and unopposed patriarch, where he unburdened himself of those crippling emotional entanglements that love and family are. And to embrace this gift is to stand in his shoes and acknowledge what he was, what he taught and what he didn't, and the great responsibilities that go with that. The motors and hardware and weather and currents, the rules and etiquette and escapades, the discipline, the patience, the silence, and the calm studied resolve.

He taught us to love the ocean. But he only taught my brother how to get there. To own this boat is to build a bridge that was never there for me.

I took paths in life never accepted by my father. I became a person he never quite understood. I discovered points of strength and beauty in myself that he never could imagine or embrace. *Can I now stand on his ground without losing my own? Can I go home to those rules and responsibilities and still find a place for the wildness of me? Can I learn to lead with a generous spirit and to teach with equanimity and to trust in my many captains, and in my many crew, and in myself as I make this crossing of peace to the ocean?*

In my life of fifty years I have made great and bitter accomplishment of my independence. I can do most things I have set my mind to do. I don't fear the dog in the fire house or the demon on the black kettle stove. I can climb a pole through a cloud and stand brittle still as the wind slices truth right out of me. I will wither flat before I scurry. But to crack this mold and part the sky, it's glorious madness, if it should be done at all, this scares me.

40

Antidotes to the Flood of Fear

by Andrea Mitchell

Majuro to Kiribati, 355 nautical miles, a short ocean passage in the North Pacific equatorial zone. A reasonably benign forecast had made leaving seem a good idea one Thursday in 2014. It turned out not so. The mysterious ITCZ (Inter-Tropical Convergence Zone) was 3,000 nm to the east near Kiritimati Island when we left Majuro. But it suddenly turned up, as it can, overnight, just after we left. Winds, predicted to be 10-15 knots for the whole trip, turned into 20-25 knots with banks of squalls adding to the excitement.

Marco the autopilot, our beloved third crew member, decided to take a holiday soon into the trip, leaving us hand-steering, two hours on, two hours off, for 36 hours. Thankfully the seas settled enough on Saturday morning for the Skipper to grab a chance to pull out Marco's control head and convince him/her that we really needed him/her back on deck! The seas between Majuro and Milli were boisterous compared to other parts of the ocean, maybe as a result of sea mounts and up-wellings, and different wave trains were moving the boat in jarring and difficult ways. Traditional pacific navigators mapped these different wave patterns to help locate themselves, and the Marshallese have lovely schematic wave charts made out of coconut battens, dotted with shells to mark the various atolls.

Still, it was exhilarating helming in the confused seas, and a really good work out for the upper arms. It certainly made us appreciate Marco a whole lot more!

The stronger-than-forecast winds and Marco's little nervous breakdown were not to be the end of our trials during that passage. Two days into our anticipated four-to-five-day journey we were into the swing of it. We had managed to cook and eat a reasonably substantial early dinner. The sun was close to going down, and darkness, not always our old friend, was deepening. It was my watch, and the Skipper was just getting ready for some shut eye when the winds started to climb again and the rapidly developing black squall to our east suddenly took over the entire sky. Reluctantly I called him back on deck. We struggled quickly into rain gear, reattached the tethers to the lifelines. We barely got the third reef in, the headsail pulled in to a handkerchief, and the storm boards in place, before we were into the gale; the heavy rain horizontal. The winds were now consistently 35-45, gusting to nearly 50 knots, with rapidly building seas.

I was not a happy camper. An acrid taste began to gather in the back of my mouth, my heart pounded wildly. All rational thought whipped away in the howling wind. Communication was almost impossible, words disappearing in the gloom, shared looks telegraphing the anxiety and building fear. We were already tired after two days of hand-steering into strong winds, but I would have given anything for the winds to drop to 25-30 knots. Already used to the yawing and gyrating of the last two days, our poor monohull was well and truly heeled over, moving insanely, as I tried to steer a course to spill the wind. The moderate sounds of our small yacht banging to windward turned into a berserk raging crashing dissonance, jangling my nerves more at each unexpected and unexplained noise. *How was the rigging holding up, what about that spreader, had a sail torn? Would the Skipper get back to the cockpit safely, what on earth was he doing up there, what was taking so long?*

And then it happened, I accidently put the boat into a heave-to position, sheets tangling and catching on the foredeck. Things became blurry after that, a momentary blank, as the Skipper returned and took over the helm – shock and anxiety freezing out the possibility of acting. I don't remember how I got there, but I found myself crouching, tethered on the cockpit floor, my eyes shut tight – as terrified as I have ever been in my life, yelling, screaming loudly, as each new gust hit. After a few long minutes of self-absorbed venting I dared to open my eyes and make sure my precious Skipper was still at the helm. There he was, ensuring we stayed heaved-to, doing what had to be done. He looked at me and smiled.

'We're okay.' Or at least that's what I thought he said before I closed my eyes again.

With the boat stabilised I was eventually able to keep my eyes open, realising that it was harder just hearing the noises and not seeing what was going on. I even remember watching the awesome, powerful, beauty of the huge waves effortlessly lifting our small home. We were still hove-to, sort of... the winds settling into consistent 35-40 knots. We were able to talk, or rather shout above the noise, about what had to happen next. I needed to take back the helm; he needed to go forward to disentangle a snagged headsail sheet to get the boat sailing again. There was no one else on board, it had to be me, unless I wanted to go forward while he helmed. Several deep breaths later, some reassuring words from the Skipper, and a bit of internal self-talk, I took back the helm so he could go forward.

I have decided I don't like winds above 40 knots at night, (daytime is not so bad), and four years on from that passage, and with more ocean passages under my belt, I still have work to do on my 'fear management strategy'. I think of all those amazing antipodean women solo sailors, Kay Cottee, Jessica Watson, Lisa Blair, who have always inspired me, my private soothing mantra being, *'if they can do it, so can I'*. And I am not even sailing alone! One of Lisa Blair's blogs was comforting, her admission that winds over 50 knots in a trans-Tasman crossing temporarily reduced her to tears before she knuckled back down to managing the boat. That was before her epic solo Antarctic circumnavigation.

I know I need to keep learning, keep working on my boat handling skills and confidence. To keep building my faith in myself, my partner, and our strong ocean-going haven. I know my fear is normal, but I can't let it paralyse me, I can't let fear flood through me.

Wet from the rain and rogue waves, we were still bouncing and crashing through the gradually calming seas. It was 11 pm before we were able to relax again as the winds came back down to a steady 25 knots. We were still heavily reefed down, with more squalls in the offing. Despite the good strong sailing winds, the rough seas meant we couldn't take advantage of the conditions to race on to Tarawa, and so we settled into a slow but steady 3-4 knots for the rest of the night, before eventually becoming becalmed and drifting for five-to-six hours. Such are the vagaries of wind.

While routinely checking the boat's power systems we realised the wind generator had blown its 'foo foo' valve, probably during the peak storm gusts. We had been too focussed on getting the sails reefed to remember to turn it off, and it was now whirling aimlessly, making an ominous clanking. With raining overcast skies, and no solar power input, we had to shepherd our on-board power very carefully to ensure enough power for navigation equipment and other vital boat functions. All through the trip we were reporting – morning and night – over the HF radio to the Majuro and Vanuatu cruiser nets, so at least someone knew where we were, and what conditions we were experiencing. More importantly, those fantastic volunteer nets provided a daily and very reassuring connection to friendly calm voices with weather updates and locations of other boats underway. Knowing we were not alone and hearing others enduring similar conditions buoyed our tired spirits.

Once we had passed Butaritari the ITCZ influence decreased and we were blessed with a lovely sunny sail back into Betio, Tarawa, reviving both us and the onboard power levels. Check-in all went smoothly and by 7.30 pm Monday night we were safely at anchor, grateful to be back in sight of land, our wind generator fixed thanks to a replacement fuse.

Why do I get scared sometimes when sailing, or anytime? Why does fear lurk beneath the watery surface of each voyage, sometimes each day? Because nature can be powerful, the sea unforgiving. Because life can be dangerous, because you can get hurt, physically and emotionally, or because, worst of all, you can lose loved ones, maybe even die.

But as long as I can live and love, I must keep building 'dikes of courage'. Being out there is worth it, sailing is worth it, being with the ones you love doing something you love is worth it.

Bio: Andrea started actual sailing in her late 40s, after years of reading all about it. Starting out as a bay sailor, it was 2011 before she braved a blue water crossing from the Philippines to Darwin with her DH (Dear Heart). She currently co-owns a 1983 38 ft C&C Landfall – *Irish Melody*, which has travelled far more nautical miles and crossed many more oceans than she has.
https://www.sailblogs.com/member/irishmelody/

41

Facing Your Fears

by Jane Jarratt

Fears? When I first started sailing I had no fears, mainly because I didn't have a clue what I was doing and lacked any imagination. I thought we'd be just going around the bay, maybe do a bit of anchoring for lunch, perhaps go alongside the odd jetty to visit an interesting town. Nothing scary about that. We were planning a 'big trip' sometime in the future but that was way off. I had plenty of time to learn how to sail before then.

Then a few of our friends became ill and died way too young. You know, in their 40s or 50s when they should have had at least 30 more years! A heart attack, a rare cancer of something, a ridiculous blood clot that never should have happened. We sat on a train one day and said, 'What if it's one of us next time? What if we hadn't done the things we want to do? What if all our dreams end up for nothing?' Six months later we were boarding our own yacht in St Maarten in the Caribbean with a year off work to sail her back to Australia.

It was all very easy at first. A short sail out around the bay, day hops from one beautiful island to the next beautiful island, anchoring overnight in glorious bays in clear, green water. Our first overnight sail was from St Maarten to Antigua and I was too occupied being seasick to worry about anything else. I just wanted to either die immediately or Get Off This Boat!

Then we attended a radio course. The instructor was a jolly fellow. He told us an allegedly true story about a couple sailing together and the man having to go up the mast to mend the radio aerial. He clipped himself on at the top, unfortunately had a heart attack and died. His wife couldn't get him down and had to sail back to port with him still up there! That's when the fears started kicking in.

We were planning to sail this boat home to Australia and I had only just done the 'anchoring for lunch' bit. *What if we were hit by a whale?*

What if we hit a container? What if we sank in a storm? What if we got knocked down (whatever that was)? What if we were boarded by pirates, taken for ransom and held in a cage and our country wouldn't pay? What if we were swimming off the back and the boat sailed away (thank you Open Water 2). What if we ate reef fish, got ciguatera and died all alone and were found weeks later? What if the boat caught fire and we had to leap overboard and watch her burn to the waterline? I could go on. There wasn't a fear I didn't take out, worry to death, and file in my brain for future reference!

Our first long trip was from the Caribbean down to Panama but, as we had two friends with us, it was an easy passage with others to share the load. We had some rough seas but nothing that I was concerned about. They left when we had transited the Canal and finally the day came for the two of us to set off on our first long passage together from Panama to the Galapagos. Just the two of us. Alone. With nobody else. I took the first watch at 9 pm and all went well. In fact, I even enjoyed it. It was a lovely calm, warm night. The sky was black, the stars were amazing, the boat was gliding through a flat, dark sea and I saw my first bio-luminescence off the stern. This was everything I could have wished for! Andy came up to relieve me at midnight and I went down to sleep. That was when a fear I hadn't even considered raised its ugly head. *'What if I go to sleep and, when I wake up and go up to the cockpit, he isn't there?'* I suddenly remembered a news story about this happening on a boat sailing up past Coffs Harbour (Australia) before we left home. And that happened during the day! Well that was it. No sleep for me. Every ten minutes I popped back up to check on him until he eventually crossly ordered me back down to bed. Then I secretly checked on him through the hatch. I could only see his feet but, if the feet were there, all was good. Then the feet vanished. I was up and out there in a flash praying to whoever might be up there watching over us 'Please let him be there! Please let him be there! Please don't let me be on my own miles from anywhere?'

He was there, of course, on the side deck fiddling with a bit of rope or something. 'What are you doing? You know the rules... You never go up on deck when the other one is sleeping!' (I'm not sure we'd made this rule, but you don't let the truth get in the way of a good argument).

'Yes, but I was only... '

'It doesn't matter what you were only...!'

'I just needed to...'

'No, you didn't! You could have waited for me to come up or called me if it was important. If I think you're going to go up there on your own, I'll never sleep again!'

Of course, he never did it again (probably) but it was some time before I ever managed to get any good sleep when off watch. Eventually sheer exhaustion took over and we fell into a pattern. This fear gradually left as did all the others. Over time, we didn't hit a container or get boarded by pirates and we learnt to watch the weather and take all the right precautions. We became more confident and the fear slowly abated leaving behind healthy minor anxiety and respect for what the sea could do.

And Andy is banned from ever going up the mast!

Bio: Jane Jarratt only started sailing in 2007 when she and her partner Andy moved from the UK to Australia. Since then they bought a boat in the St Maarten in the Caribbean, sailed it back to Sydney in 2009, and have spent the last five Northern Hemisphere summers sailing in the Med. To avoid any winters at all, they live in Scarborough in Queensland during the Southern Hemisphere summer. Jane runs the Women Who Sail the Med Facebook group and her blog can be found on https://svolive.com/

42

Om Namah Shivayah!

by Fiona McCormick

After a couple of weeks at sea the boat develops a rhythm unique to every voyage. Our ocean-crossing home was 36-feet-long, a unique hand-built haven with the cloud forms, wave-slap, and creaking rigging, our ever-changing sensory background. In rare and cherished letters, friends asked, 'What do you do all day? How to describe the cycle of watches, the meticulous timing when taking and working out sun-sights, the daily sorting through stores to prepare wholesome meals, the focus involved in anticipating and attending to wind shifts, preventive maintenance to reduce chafe – the myriad of tiny yet time-consuming actions required to ensure our safety and peace of mind?

I was on watch midnight to 0600 and midday to 1800. The night watches enabled me to turn our craft towards the rising sun for a few glorious moments every morning, singing softly the Pink Floyd lyrics, *'Set the controls for the heart of the sun,'* and really feeling the connection between the graceful arc of our sails, the subtle curve of the horizon and the sun's heated heart driving the world's wind.

By breakfast handover it was time to rouse my toddler son and well rested skipper, check our position line then head down for a kip. At midday, I would once again take on boat handling and childcare duties until we shared the evening meal, and the kerosene nav lights were filled and lit to provide us with a reassuring glow as we sailed on into the night.

Evenings were quite short due to needing to be back on watch at midnight, however there was always time to read, sew clothes for the cold weather expected ahead, read (and reread) classics such as Adlard Coles *Heavy Weather Sailing* and the accounts of navigators, from James Cook to Joshua Slocum, David Lewis to Naomi James, as well as cautionary tales such as those of the Bailey's *117 Days Adrift* and Smeeton's *Once is Enough.*

I had joined the boat in India – grateful for the opportunity to learn about sailing on this sturdy homemade Herreshoff ketch, and particularly appreciative that the skipper had no qualms about sailing with a woman and child who couldn't swim. We had no engine by intention, and the single solar panel powered batteries for the chart table light and depth sounder. A home-made self-steering device kept us on course in all but the heaviest seas. During the year of 1985 we had sailed her from India to the Chagos Archipelago, where we nearly lost her to fire one rainy night due to an error of judgement while refilling the metho bottle. On that leg, I certainly learnt I could trust our skipper to respond appropriately in a crisis! After waiting a few months for the trade winds to kick in we headed down to Mauritius, then Isle de la Réunion. We were now following a Great Circle course back to Australia, a distance of around 3,500 nm. We hoped we could break it up by calling in for a few days' rest and a feed of lobster at the submerged volcano known as Île Saint-Paul.

Île Saint-Paul lies at 77.5°E, in a direct line south from India towards Antarctica. It presents a sheer cliff face to the swells of the Southern Indian Ocean and to yachts running the downwind course approaching from the west. Day after day heavy skies prevented us from shooting a sextant sight of sun, moon, or stars, and tension was building over the accuracy of our charted positions. Were we really going to pass 50 miles north or was there a current drifting us towards this jagged tooth of land? However, as the days progressed, and our accuracy diminished, something far more ominous was brewing.

The sea bed is not like a beach: there are rift valleys deeper than Mount Everest is high, and submarine ridges down there which are several kilometres higher than the surrounding plains. One such ridge, prosaically described as the 'Mid Indian Ridge', thrusts itself 3,000 metres above the floor of the Indian Ocean to within 1,000 metres of the surface. This makes the swells shorter and steeper, much as the slope of a beach causes lazy rollers to turn into churning surf. In hindsight, it is obvious that one could expect a rougher ride, for water that has travelled thousands of kilometres over a uniformly deep ocean was suddenly funnelled upwards by this hidden landform. We went from a gentle sashay over predictably spaced rolling crests some eight seconds apart and 3-5 metres in height, to a veritable boat-washing-machine throwing us from one snarling comber to another with an exhausting jerk. With each lift, the stern tried to turn parallel with the seas and we had to hand steer for the first time since leaving Réunion, adding to our discomfort and unease.

Then the wind began to build... and build. From a steady force 6, each new log entry showed the steps taken to cope with increasingly turbulent seas as we progressively shortened sail. Sometime that afternoon I headed out along the bowsprit and unhanked the jib we'd dropped earlier so it could be stowed safely below, we weren't risking it dragging overboard and fouling our steering. As a particularly steep sea lifted the stern I glanced back at the cockpit and saw an image which remains indelibly etched in my psyche more than three decades later: the skipper, outlined against a massive wall of ocean, he and the stern metres above me. After struggling back to the relative safety of the cockpit, we talked about what to do to avoid broaching and discussed shortening our watches now we were hand steering. According to Admiral Beaufort we now had storm force 10 winds, very high waves with overhanging crests, foam blown in very dense streaks, and reduced visibility. *What visibility?* I thought to myself. There was also an unnerving high-pitched wail as the wind whistled through the rigging.

I was all for heaving-to at that stage, however the far more experienced skipper decided to continue sailing as we were still at risk of colliding with the fearsome wall of Île Saint-Paul. As I helmed us over an ocean intent on swapping places with the sky I returned to the basics. The stern would lift under my widely-braced feet and the character and direction of that lift would determine how much pressure to apply to the tiller by leaning into it with knees and thighs... and sometimes my entire body weight. It was such a relief to finally head down for a rest off-watch.

Wedged into my berth, lee cloth cocooning myself and child, the hull amplified the ferociousness of the weather. Every trough gave a temporary lull, but as we climbed the peaks the shrieking wind would suddenly fill our shred of canvas with a *T-W-A-N-G* that I was sure would dismast us. As we careened down into the next trough I held my breath – *Is this the time we broach? Where IS Île Saint-Paul anyway?*

Lull, twang, shudder, repeat.

At some stage I couldn't cope anymore and retreated into a place far removed from the hostile environment, singing a mantra that meant a lot to me: *Om Namah Shivayah*!

According to Hindu belief, at the end of each epoch Shiva dances a dance in which the universe is dissolved, so that a new one can rise from the fire of his dance. It seemed particularly apt on this darkest and most chaotic of nights to honour that renewal. I was certain that on the next *T-W-A-N-G* our rigging would fail, and the mast would fall, we would lose steerage and broach. Or that brave man out there would lose focus and we'd turn side on to the mountainous seas. Or we'd meet Île Saint-Paul with a crash. This was it. I knew I would not survive to sing to the rising sun. On the bright side, I would die doing what I loved most; voyaging across oceans. However, there would be a permanent hole in the Universe as I would have caused the death of my precious boy, and my young daughter would experience the same loss, and possibly the same self-inflicted trauma that had plagued me since my mother died too early.

Surrendering to the ocean was easy, it is what sailing is all about and I'd had plenty of practice! Fortunately, at midnight the skipper decided we should heave-to, although the snarling combers were scary, and I was fighting with all my strength to hold us on our invisible course while he fixed the sails so we'd be able to turn and heave-to when we found a lull. The rest of that night passed in relative comfort and we survived. WE SURVIVED... and even thrived, secure that we'd ridden out our once-in-a-voyage storm and our well-found boat was up for whatever the ocean could throw at us.

Bio: In my 20s I voyaged from India to Australia and decided to become a GP so I could venture out on the ocean aboard my own yacht and travel to destinations in the Pacific with a useful skillset to offer once I got there. This took more than 25 years, so you can imagine my elation to be sailing north to Stradbroke Island to work in an Aboriginal Medical Service in my 50s!

43

Passage

by Jeannie Richter Conn

As we rounded the end of Cape May in *Montserrat*, I was excited and afraid, I couldn't wait, and I couldn't breathe. I'd never been on the ocean.

All day, as we calmly motor-sailed down Delaware Bay, I waited for Peter to finish settling the boat into its rhythm and provide some tips and some idea of what to expect.

My stomach felt tight, my mind full of questions. Everyone's advice ran through my head, but I didn't put much stock in what anyone else had to say, I'd been waiting for Peter's guidance. Still Peter said nothing. I felt a growing resentment. Our communication styles were completely different. I talked. He didn't.

It was late afternoon, the sun still hot and high in the sky, hours to go until sunset. As we approached the tip of Cape May and saw the lighthouse, I looked at Peter with some contempt. I snapped photographs and tried to stay cheerful. As the waves began to rock the boat, I put down the camera in favor of my harness. Dad's advice, harkening back to his Coast Guard Auxiliary days, and his fear of rogue waves was, 'Stay clipped on, no matter what.' I knew falling off a boat offshore meant almost certain death.

I fumbled with the carabiner that held the clips together. It was a struggle with the constant motion of the boat and I hadn't even connected to the jacklines Peter had run from the bow to the cockpit. We were taking the shortest route north and that meant navigating through the narrow channel off the coast of Cape May instead of going out farther, leaving a wide berth for the shoals off the cape.

Suddenly Peter shouted to check the chart plotter for the depth. Not knowing the seriousness of what could happen to the boat as we passed through the channel if we strayed even a little outside, I continued to fumble with the carabiner.

More shouting, 'What are you doing? I need you to focus on the chart right now. I need your help.'

'Stop shouting at me! My life is more important than running aground!'

I did not realize that running aground here was nothing like the soft landing on mud that we'd done too many times in the river and bay. Hitting the craggy rocks below would rip up *Montserrat's* hull leaving us shipwrecked. I shouted to him from the nav station below to tell him where we were and which way to turn to keep us in the channel. After a few minutes that seemed like hours, we made it through the channel.

Twenty minutes later, the waves grew bigger and with each one the sailboat rolled side-to-side. If I didn't finish putting everything away it would soon be flying everywhere. Even now, that's the thing I don't like about sailing – when the contents below crash every time we tack or when waves roll the boat.

I stowed every last item and set up the cushions and linens, so that the bed was ready for the off-watch person to get some sleep as we worked our way up the coast for the next two days. After fighting the gravity of pitching and rolling in that hot cabin, I felt queasy. I never usually suffered with seasickness, I must have some weird badge of honor, but I also knew the best way to fight an onset of queasiness was to get out to fresh air and look at the horizon.

I put on the harness and pulled myself up. In the ocean, this feels a little like mountain climbing even though it's only two steps. I braced against the companionway while I clipped the carabiner onto the jackline and then tried to relax in the cockpit as Peter made me a drink. All the pressure, the tense gaiety of the day finally caught up to me. Peter handed up a ginger ale and rum to settle my stomach.

Now bolstered by the rum, I tried to explain to Peter. 'You keep saying that there's no way to know until you do it, but…'

'I just don't think it's a big deal.'

'It is to me. The whole time leading up to the trip, we were both so busy getting ready we didn't even have time to really talk about the trip. I know that. I just figured we'd have lots of time today for you to impart all your wisdom and tips, but instead you've been tight-lipped all day. Every time I tried to start the conversation, you ridiculed me!'

'I didn't ridi…'

'You did! I asked you something about the night watch and you just brushed it off. And everyone else had given me their advice and I listened politely. But you're the only one I really trust. You're the one who's been out here the most of anyone. I just figured that's what today was going to be.'

It was normal for me to do most of the talking, but I saw by the look on Peter's face that he finally got it – *I was afraid.* He softened, reassuring me that of course I was going to have fears, that was all part of it, but really it was no big deal. We were safe, the boat was safe, the weather looked perfect, everything would be fine, and we'd be at Block Island in about 46 hours.

We ate dinner in the cockpit – chili that Peter made – and decided that because I'm a night owl, I would take the first watch from sunset until one in the morning, giving Peter about four hours' sleep.

In the last blue violet light of day, I looked over the ocean and felt a tremendous sense of space. How unfathomable, how vast.

As darkness took over, I looked up and felt childlike wonder and delight. The stars, invisible moments before, became vibrant, pulsing and twinkling like sparklers frozen in that enormous blue sky. I remembered the next day was the 4th of July. We were 20 miles offshore, angling out toward Block Island, still another 200 miles to sail. On my watch, I sat in the cockpit close to the companionway, and looked back at the tiny lights on-shore. I noticed red lights, fireworks from a seaside town, then there were so many I couldn't count them all, up and down the coast in all the towns where people went to celebrate Independence Day. They looked like brake lights in a traffic jam; I watched from a watery distance.

I spent my first night watch at sea in awe. The power of the ocean and waves is undeniable. When I looked into the darkness of the water, the waves as they rolled the little sailboat, I reasoned the way I always do when I'm worried. I told myself that I would be okay, that I still had important work to do, that surely this could not be my end. I made promises, I made deals, like we do when we're really scared of something.

My fears called into question everything that I believed about positive thinking and how the right thoughts and right actions played into my fate. In those hours, I came to realize beyond doubt that no amount of thinking can really change anything. I'm not actually in control – of anything. I am just a speck, just a drop in that proverbial ocean. I prayed to God for the first time in a long while. There was no over intellectualizing God here, no doubting whether God exists. You're sure. You have to be.

After a few hours, my jacket damp from spray and dew, I crawled down the steps to the cabin and shook Peter awake. The next morning, I took the helm for a few hours. During the day, the sea was calm. We chatted, made meals, and almost caught a fish. At night, the breeze and waves returned. Once darkness took over the second night, I was ready for the black depths and rolling waves. I was willing to accept the uncertainty and even more enthralled by the beauty of sailing on the ocean at night.

By Monday evening, we'd traded watches a few times, and were in sight of Montauk Point, across the sound from Block Island. We'd made it safely on my first ocean trip. The boat had not run into any serious trouble. Not yet anyway. The fears I had were in my own head. Facing them didn't mean a greater sense of control, but more ease with not being in control.

I've since sailed many miles in the ocean on boats with Peter. We've faced scary moments with engines failing, storms at sea, even a boat taking on water 250 miles offshore of Nicaragua. What I learned that first night at sea has stayed with me. There is grace in not knowing, not controlling it all. And *inshallah*, we'll have many more moments on this astonishing, powerful ocean.

44

How to Sink a Narrowboat

by Jill Budd

I'd like to say it was an accident, but I only have myself to blame. I made a mistake and I should have been carrying a knife. With a good lawyer I might have claimed, 'mitigating circumstances' in my defence.

For six years, we had cruised the Inland Waterways of England and Wales on our narrowboat, and we both had our 60th birthdays and our 25th wedding anniversary approaching. With no family left on my side, we thought that the best way to spend our celebratory money would be to ship the narrowboat across the pond and explore pastures 'foreign'.

Despite our years of cruising, we had very little experience of rope handling in locks, let alone locks that are controlled by something or someone else and not even necessarily in the same vicinity. The basic locking procedure for a narrowboat on a narrow canal in the UK is to leave it in gear on the top gate and let it ride up as you slowly open the paddles – downhill it matters not at all; no ropes required.

Having been in Belgium for only six weeks I felt way out of my comfort zone. I spoke very little of the local lingo; we carried only a small water tank and were living with the constant worry that we would run out of water. I had been almost dragged off the tiller by the sheer amount of water being sucked from under me as huge commercial boats overtook us. Worse still was that we struggled to find calm moorings away from the rock 'n' roll caused by passing shipping. And the dogs were becoming very unhappy. In short, I was pretty close to suggesting that we go back to the UK. If we hadn't arrived (and been travelling) with friends on their boat, I think I would have gone back with my tail under my tiller arm.

On this particular day, near the Strepy-Thieu lift, we entered a lock with a three metre drop directly behind our friends' boat; both just squeezing in nicely. There was no reachable bollard for me to put the bow rope on, so I slotted it through a rung on the escape ladder, lifted the blue 'start' rod and watched the gates behind close. As the lock emptied, I started to pay out the rope around the ladder rung and realised I couldn't – it was snagged in a weld on the ladder.

I shall live forever with that terrifying sound of a creaking rope under the massive strain of 20 tonnes of narrowboat without the water to support it.

I couldn't free the rope and the lock kept emptying. I lifted the emergency stop red alarm rod, pulled it, twisted it and, probably, bent it; but still the water kept going down. By now the bow was suspended, the stern counter was starting to go under, and I was screaming like a fishwife. My skipper was 'climbing' along the narrow gunwales towards me as my friend, on the boat in front, shot down into his galley and grabbed a knife shouting, 'Stand back and I'll throw the knife onto you'.

Skipper grabbed the knife first and touched the rope which broke immediately under the strain and we splashed back on the water in a horizontal position. The horrendous creaking noise stopped and suddenly it was deathly quiet.

I shot into the boat to check on the animals; only to find the dogs paddling about happily in olive oil, mayonnaise, broken glass, and china. The cat was in her normal position – fast asleep on our bed. Then it hit me. I shook violently for about twenty minutes; not helped by my Skipper pronouncing the obvious, 'Do you realise how close we were to sinking – another 30 seconds and she'd have been under?'

I heard a tiny voice – mine apparently – say 'A hug would be nice, I've had enough, I want to go back to the UK, I can't do this anymore.'

We didn't go back; we learnt.

I now carry more knives than the average troop of boy scouts and won't go near a lock without them – the knives that is; not the scouts. Five years on and, I confess, my blood pressure still rises a little on every lock approach.

Bio: I was fortunate enough to take early retirement at the age of 54; selling my craft shops and moving onto a narrowboat to cruise the British inland waterways with my husband, two dogs, and two cats. After 6 years, we shipped the narrowboat across to mainland Europe and loved it so much that we stayed; selling the narrowboat and buying an elderly Dutch Barge. We still continue to cruise throughout Europe and you can follow our travels on my blog *contentedsouls.com*

45

Curiosity Killed the Fear

by Renee Smith

Everyone knows that despite their supposed nine lives, curiosity kills cats. What is lesser known though is that curiosity can kill another beast with nine lives that is just as savage and cunning as your average big cat. Curiosity can kill fear.

We'll join this true story at the place where I was in the oddest of friendships with two teenage sisters. How we ever became such good friends I don't know, because other than the three of us all being female, I had nothing in common with them. I had a physical disability and was a wheelchair user – they were fit, active, always on the go, and highly capable. I was a keen and accomplished equestrian – they didn't like horses at all. They were keen and accomplished sailors – I had a strong, life-long, dislike of boats. I loved land – they loved being on the water. I know they say opposites attract, but I mean really – have you ever tried to have a conversation with someone when you literally have no idea what they are talking about?

As it turned out, having some close friends with a totally different lifestyle to yourself can be lifesaving. When my health condition deteriorated further, my medical team made the difficult decision that forced me to end my equestrian career. Becoming a full-time supporter of my friends' competitive sailing careers kept me busy and far away from everything horse related. I had no time to be affected by my great loss. I was too busy with either travelling up and down the coast to various regattas or Googling the definition of every second word that came out of their mouths. And it's hard to stay heart broken when the younger one in her hot pink gear can be clearly heard laughing loudly and screaming with happiness, as she's bow down and sending it out to the start line*.

I hadn't envisioned one rather large problem though. No more equestrian career meant that they were safely able to start badgering me to hop on a sailing vessel without the threat of having to hop on a horse themselves, in an, 'I'll try yours if you try mine' kind of arrangement. I was exposed and powerless.

The only thing stopping me was the fear associated with my history on any, and all, boating craft. Any boating trip would end with me being nauseous or seasick. Even the ever so slight rocking of a Manly Ferry still tied up at Circular Quay, or just standing on a floating dock, was enough to get my head spinning. I wasn't afraid of seasickness itself – I feared what came with it – becoming the centre of attention or making a fool of myself. Everyone immediately looks at the person who is different, there's no way to blend in with the crowd anymore, and I really hate not being able to get it right like everyone else. But outwardly claiming that I didn't want to go sailing because I always used to get seasick was much easier than admitting what my real fears were.

The months went by, the faithful badgering to try sailing continued, and my controlling fears were still very real. One thing was slowly changing though – my curiosity was growing. It grew each time one of the sisters would tag me in some epic offshore sailing footage that I needed to watch on Facebook, or the messenger chats we would have at some odd hour at night as we commentated the live regatta footage we were watching. It grew with the focus and skill I'd capture in every photograph I took of them competing, and the salty, windswept hairstyles they'd return to the shore with, as well as the smiles and light in their eyes as they animatedly recounted the happenings of each close race. No one says it better than the pirate himself, Captain Jack Sparrow – *"You will come over to my side, I know it… One word love, curiosity. You long for freedom. You long to do what you want to do because you want it, to act on selfish impulse. You want to see what it's like. One day, you won't be able to resist."*

And he was right – one day, I wasn't able to resist my ever-growing curiosity any longer, and I found myself putting my name down on the guest list to try sailing with the Sailors with disABILITIES not-for-profit organisation that sailed out of the same marina that the older of the sisters did. I had no idea what I was doing, nor could I believe what I was doing. About the only intelligent and logical thought I had was that if one morning out on the water with this group of strangers didn't go well for me and seasickness lead me to feeling those things I feared, it's not like I would ever have to see any of them again and keep reliving my fears. I could satisfy my curiosity and say that I tried.

I was a woman still totally engulfed in curiosity as my friend drove me into the marina – I wasn't anxious, wasn't nervous. You'd think that I might have some nerves, even if they were simply about how I'd go about getting around the yacht as an incomplete paraplegic. But no – I have no fear when it comes to my view of myself and my physical ability. It's interactions with people that I fear, but like I said, I was a woman totally engulfed in curiosity. I was barely aware of all the strangers around as my friend wheeled me up a ramp and onto the deck of a 54-foot yacht. I didn't notice the eyes on me as I transferred out of my chair, onto the deck, and started sliding myself around to look at everything. I barely even paused to say goodbye to my friend as she wheeled my chair back off the boat for me, parked it on the dock, and then hung around in the background for a little while to make sure I was okay. I was totally engrossed in curiosity.

What happened out there for those few hours that I was sailing around Sydney Harbour and out of The Heads to experience a little bit of the ocean and that big, blue horizon, I don't really know, and I can't really describe to you. But during those few hours, as my friend was provision shopping and packing the yacht she was sailing on for an ocean race beginning in just a few days, she kept thinking about me, wondering how I was going, and worrying when the breeze picked up. She happened to be up on deck when she spied the yacht she had dropped me off to, motoring back in towards the marina. Jumping off her yacht and hurrying over to the berth we would be docking in, she was waiting there as the helmsman turned into the channel. In the first instance when she saw my face she knew that I was more than alright. She saw my face and tears began to appear in her eyes. Without me having to say anything, she knew I had been hooked. She knew that I now understood. She knew that this moment was just the first in what would become a big journey of sailing, self-healing and growth.

And the stories I've collected so far, that are a part of my ever-expanding journey of sailing, are for another day. The point of this story is just this – curiosity killed the fear. To this day, I still haven't been able to resist it – I still long to taste the freedom that sailing brings, there are still so many things that I want to see and understand. My sailing journey is still engulfed in curiosity. Every time I am lifted onto the deck, the fears and anxieties that are there in my daily life cannot follow me on board.

Now, when I go to take others with disabilities or disadvantages out on our special yachts, if someone is being attacked by nerves and fears, I slide my way across the deck to them, until I'm right up close. With a lowered voice, I recite my own version of the Captain Jack Sparrow curiosity quote. *"You know what I think will happen? You will get out there on the harbour and experience something amazing. Then you will have your chance to do something, something courageous. You won't be able to resist. You're going to want to know what it feels like…"*.

*Bow down and sending it out to the start line. Racing term – giving it all she's got!

Bio: Renee is an incomplete paraplegic, MS patient, and adaptive sailor from Sydney, Australia. She had her first experience on a yacht, and was shown the freedom sailing could offer, through the not-for-profit organisation Sailors with disABILITIES (SWD) in mid-2017. Since that first addictive exposure, her weekly routine now involves fitting as much sailing as possible around her research career in plant physiology. As a crew volunteer with SWD's programs, Renee trades her wheelchair in for a 54-foot racing yacht and takes groups of kids and adults who have a disability or disadvantage out on Sydney Harbour for a sailing experience that focuses on ability, optimism, confidence and achievement. Renee is also a member of SWD's racing team, crewing weekly in harbour race series and regattas, and is working towards offshore racing. Outside of this weekly routine, she enjoys supporting her friends in their dinghy or yacht racing careers, and photographing regattas and offshore races.
Instagram: @toby_renee_adventuring

46

Embracing Fear: The Birth of an Ocean Gypsy

by Kristen Anderson

Several years ago, I experienced a darkly powerful and defining moment in my life. It was a moment of extreme fear, and it was also a moment that launched a remarkable journey of intense discovery. There are, it turns out, many things in life to fear, and trying to define, understand, and come to terms with them led to much questioning. The search for answers explored previously untraveled paths, opened many new doors, and delivered adventure, perspective, and clarity. This moment occurred aboard the yacht *Commitment* as she suffered a heavy knock-down sailing back to Chile after the adventure of a lifetime in Antarctica. Embracing the fears it unleashed has been life-changing.

It was the 23rd of February 2016. We were deep in the treacherous Southern Ocean, 200 nautical miles from the Antarctic continent, 350 nautical miles south off Cape Horn, in those horror-story latitudes known as the Screaming Sixties. The wind, gale force and building, was indeed screaming, and the seas, ominously streaked with white, had begun to turn mountainous. They were now around the size of three to four-story buildings and continuing to grow. We were taking breaking waves into the cockpit. The auto pilot refused to hold, and helming was strenuous and dangerous. Our situation was becoming increasingly alarming and the decision was made to heave-to, bunker down and hope to ride it out.

The storm continued to rage. Night fell, black and angry, and the world outside our tiny sanctuary grew more terrifying by the minute. Cold, wet, and frightened, I was lying in my bunk listening to the deafening chaos, flinching with terror each time we were violently slewed or slammed by ferocious breakers, wondering how much *Commitment* could withstand, trying in vain to stay calm. And then it happened... A titanic rogue wave took us broadside, and dragged us up its monstrous face, up and up... and up... and up. Before I could even brace for impact we neared its crest, which broke on top of us with thunderous force and hurled us, free-falling, deep into the cavernous trough below. Then, above the roaring, foaming and hissing of the water and the ear-splitting screeching of the wind, there was a crash I imagined to be like two freight trains colliding at great speed. I was instantly flipped over, my face pressed into hard timber, and I was pinned! I was pinned by the force of water, freezing two-degree Antarctic water! I was submerged in water. I couldn't breathe. I thought then and there – *this is it... life is over...*

Word meaning searches describe fear as an 'unpleasant emotion' caused by some sort of awareness of 'danger, pain or harm'. When we recall moments of intense fear, like the one I have just described, 'unpleasant', seems entirely inadequate and a gross understatement! *How do you come to terms with the type of 'unpleasantness' that won't go away, threatens to completely unbalance you, and prevents you from doing the very things you love?* I was told that many people, after such severe knock-downs, never set foot on boats again, and I felt it highly likely that I would be one of them. For many months, attempts to sleep on board (without even leaving the dock!) resulted in extreme panic attacks that had me fleeing the boat in a blind and all-consuming terror, gasping for air. Fear found me in my dreams, both waking and asleep, and paralysed me. There was no logic to it. Where was the reason for it when there was no longer any imminent danger, pain, or harm? I feared that I might never overcome this fear. I was spiralling and the 'unpleasantness' multiplied. This couldn't continue and had to be faced.

And so, the questioning began. What was it that I was afraid of? Was it the ocean, was it the knockdown, or was it something else, something less tangible? When that rogue wave tossed 32-tonne Commitment as though she were nothing more than a piece of driftwood, life as I had known it ceased to exist. The outrageous winds and horrific seas lasted another twelve hours – a long time in a damaged boat in the middle of the Southern Ocean to think about your mortality. 'Life is short,' had, until then, been simply a much-quoted, corny cliché. But upside down in that bunk, believing the cabin top had torn off and life was done and dusted, that little cliché had become a mantra. So what,

I asked myself, safely back on land, donning my corporate uniform for yet another day scrabbling around the nine-to-five wheel, was I doing with it? My mind dreamed of pristine Antarctic wilderness and soared with majestic albatross to endless horizons. It remembered perfect freedom and the glorious rhythm of the ocean even as my body crunched numbers on spreadsheets and plodded in to meaningless meetings.

Back in this mundane world, what were those waking nightmares really all about? Did I think I was going to die? Or was I afraid that I wasn't really living? Was it the fear of going back to sea or of the continued monotony of a commercial profit-and-loss world I no longer believed in?

Commitment didn't sink to the bottom of the Southern Ocean, she righted herself. She was wounded but we limped her back to Chile relatively intact, her crew physically unharmed. *Why all the emotional upheaval?*

Fast forward twelve months and *Commitment* was coming home to Australia. One phone call, asking, 'Did I want to be on board?' and the puzzle pieces came together. I had my answers! The truth was that, whilst I had been given the gift of life, I was not treating it with the respect such a solemn gift deserved. I was not being true to some deep but unspoken exchange. I resigned from work, rented out my home, put my possessions in storage and, wet weather gear and sea-boots in hand, boarded a plane on a one-way ticket to Chile.

Was I completely insane? Perhaps, and certainly there were many who thought so ('Mum, people your age don't just run off and have gap years!'). But I was listening to that 'life-is-short' refrain, honouring that precious gift and, at the age of 53, I was about to do some serious living.

Of course, the prospect of four months at sea was not without its fears. But more terrifying than any ocean crossing was the belated reality that I was walking away from a perfectly good job… turning a determinedly blind eye to the mortgage and just, for the first time since commencing work at the steelworks at the tender age of 17, chucking it in. *This* was indeed a leap, and one that produced some serious 'punch-in-the-guts' fear. *What if no-one will employ me when I get back? What if the tenants leave? How will I pay the mortgage?* And, while we're at it, let's question the sanity of sailing the South Pacific!

What if we get that same weather again? Get knocked down again? What if we lose the mast this time? What if, what if, what if?

Aaarrrghhhhhhhh!

But, as I had discovered in the post-Antarctica 'year of questioning', fear in itself is not to be feared. This new fear was no different, I just had to understand it and embrace it. *What was it that I was so frightened of?* The danger here lay only in me, in a lack of confidence. This was, for me, ground-breaking territory, and I was, purely and simply, afraid of failing. So, I made a conscious choice to believe in myself and, just like magic, the panic subsided. I backed myself that when the need for money arose, I would find it, and I backed myself that even though I didn't consider myself much of a sailor, I would find one within, and in an extraordinary four-month journey covering over 8,000 nautical miles, I experienced adventure I could barely have imagined, found courage I wasn't sure I possessed and discovered the peace and serenity to be found in the smallest of pleasures. And the real prize? What an astonishingly liberating thing it is to have reclaimed my life, to be living it for me and mine instead of a corporation, to unchain from the grind of the working wheel while I still harbour dreams and my body is fit and agile and strong enough to make them a reality!

And the journey hasn't ended. Eighteen months on, 'Gap Year the Sequel' is showing every sign of becoming a trilogy and I am still the happiest of ocean gypsies. To say I am pleased to have faced those fears at a defining time in my life is the understatement of the century! And more importantly, I continue to face them. We will always encounter things we fear, and the more vividly we live our lives, the more numerous they will be. So, embrace them and enjoy where they take you! Oh, and I hope they take you sailing!

Bio: Kris has been sailing for around 10 years and enjoys both racing and cruising. She has raced with SheSAILS@NCYC all-female crews for several years and is a passionate advocate for women's sailing. She also sails regularly with mixed crews and particularly enjoys the longer offshore races, including Southport and Hobart. Kris considers herself fortunate to have had some extraordinary cruising opportunities that have changed her life. After a knock-down en route from Antarctica in 2016 she traded the corporate world for the life of an Ocean Gypsy and has since cruised through Patagonia, crossed the South Pacific from Chile to Australia, set sail for Lord Howe for a barbeque and joined the cruising nomads on the Australian East Coast. She has written several short stories about her adventures, which can be found online under 'Kris Anderson Ocean Gypsy', and is available for motivational speaking, where her 'Just Say Yes' philosophy and zest for life offers an inspirational message.

Acknowledgements

We would like to thank all the wonderful and talented authors who contributed to this anthology. Your passion and honesty is overwhelming. You've helped create an extraordinary book that not only is a great read, but a practical guide to help others. Most importantly, by laying open your very souls you have shown us all that we are never alone in our fears.

We'd also like to thank the brilliant and keen-eyed beta-readers who assisted in polishing the final draft. We are indebted to your care in helping us produce a professional publication.

Reviews
Please help more readers find Facing Fear Head On, by leaving a brief review on the website where you purchased this book. Many thanks.

SisterShip Magazine is under the SisterShip Press Pty Ltd umbrella. We publish the first global magazine written by women for women on the water.

Our bi-monthly, digital publication can be viewed here: https://issuu.com/sistershipmagazine

SisterShip Magazine's ethos:

Belong: Share passions with like-minded people;
Encourage: Support women, assist, advise, share, trust;
Inspire: Creating ideas, thoughts, hopes, dreams;
Inform: Promote safety, topical, newsy, fresh, detail; and
Entertain: Be exciting, new, fun, rich, safe, honest, reliable.

We'd love you to join us on our journey.

Best wishes,

Shelley and Jackie

www.sistershipmagazine.com
www.sistershippress.com
editor@sistershipmagazine.com
Twitter: @SisterShipMag
Instagram: @sistershipmagazine
Facebook: SisterShip Magazine, SisterShip Press, SisterShip Book Club